THIS BRITAIN

THIS BRITAIN

Tradition and Achievement

EDITED BY NEWTON BRANCH

Essay Index Reprint Series

BOOKS FOR LIBRARIES PRESS
FREEPORT, NEW YORK

Copyright © 1951 by Harper & Row, Publishers, Inc.

Reprinted 1970 by arrangement

STANDARD BOOK NUMBER:
8369-1549-6

LIBRARY OF CONGRESS CATALOG CARD NUMBER:
79-90612

PRINTED IN THE UNITED STATES OF AMERICA

CONTENTS

FOREWORD by Compton Mackenzie : page 5

Chapter 1 THIS SCEPTRED ISLE by Michael Lewis : page 7

Chapter 2 LANDSCAPE WITH FIGURES by L.A.G.Strong : page 14

Chapter 3 THE ENGLISH SCENE by Osbert Lancaster : page 27

Chapter 4 DOWN TO EARTH by The Earl of Portsmouth : page 37

Chapter 5 THE CRAFTSMEN by Bernard Hollowood : page 44

Chapter 6 HEART OF FIRE by Roy Lewis : page 64

Chapter 7 THE MIDDLE WAY by The Viscount Hailsham : page 77

Chapter 8 THE AMATEURS by Nigel Balchin : page 85

Chapter 9 THE GLORY OF THE WORD by Ivor Brown : page 96

Chapter 10 THE FANATICS by Stephen Potter : page 109

Chapter 11 WE ARE AMUSED by Paul Jennings : page 125

Chapter 12 THE PAGEANT by William Glenvil Hall : page 136

ACKNOWLEDGEMENTS : page 152

FOREWORD

by Compton Mackenzie

I venture to suggest that there will hardly be a reader of *This Britain* who will not have to admit when he has turned the last page how ignorant he himself is of his own country. *This Britain* does not pretend to be a work of topography; and that is all to the good, because any kind of guide book to places or counties or districts should be the work of a single hand if it is to avoid misleading the guided by the advice of various people, each of whom has his own criterion for what is beautiful or interesting. The twelve essays that make up *This Britain* deal with aspects of life in our country rather than with aspects of the natural scene. Nevertheless, each one in its own way demands that the reader shall supply the background, and that is where the reader's familiarity with the natural scene will be tested.

I should not have found Lord Portsmouth's lucid account of our livestock breeds quite so enthralling if I had not been able to conjure to the mind's eye the landscapes in which they grazed or routed. I should not have found Mr. Bernard Hollowood's or Mr. Roy Lewis's essays on industry so absorbing if I had not paid many a visit to the scenes of light and heavy industry where the men and women whom they evoke so vividly work. Yet, lest I should seem to be setting myself up as ubiquitous, let me confess that at the moment of writing I have seen every cathedral in England and Wales except Canterbury.

And having made that humiliating confession I feel I can without impertinence express a hope that readers will regard *This Britain* as a prelude to the exploration of their own country.

The task of a Foreword writer is the least enviable that literature can inflict: before I find myself in a morass of platitudes I will offer my old friend Ivor Brown what I consider the best run of monosyllables in the English language, and at the same time a couplet I believe well fitted for the exit of a Foreword writer:

'Since there's no help, come let us kiss and part,
Nay, I have done: you get no more of me.'

1
THIS SCEPTRED ISLE

By Michael Lewis

It was a Yorkshire carpenter who, in competition with all the brains of the world, discovered how to measure longitude, and so to navigate the seas with security. It was through Greenwich, and not Paris or New York, that the Meridian accepted by all came to run. It was in a London coffee-house that a practical, and equitable, risk-sharing scheme was worked out for all the world's ship-owners. It was the back-rooms of Britain wherein quiet men developed that marvel, invaluable no less for peace than for war, Radar.

Why? Why – each time – Britain? Because we had the natural bent for such things, and the natural need: because, for long years, we had found it useful, in the ordinary run of life, to go steadily to work along such lines: and – most important of all – because through long centuries we were left to ourselves to develop these needs of ours in our own way, without the dictation of foreign rulers, or the heavy footfall of foreign armies.

History does not repeat itself, even though historians do. Yet, the world over, similar effects are apt to flow from similar causes, leaving certain *lessons* of history, which our governors will ignore at their peril – and at ours. What history bids us remember, first and all the time, is the sea: how, for centuries, it – and nowadays its natural corollary, the air – have served us faithfully, and in a double capacity: for defence, and for offence.

> '... this scepter'd isle,
> This earth of majesty, this seat of Mars,
> This other Eden, demi-paradise ...
> This precious stone set in the silver sea,
> Which serves it in the office of a wall,
> Or as a moat defensive to a house ...'

We must not exaggerate of course, nor imagine that all our rulers (the real John of Gaunt amongst them) have been informed with such insight all the time, or maintained continuously our defensive walls, whether of skins or wood, iron, steel or aluminium (but never, observe, of stone). There have been long and alarming gaps when such consciousness was so dormant as to look completely dead; when

Left: The figurehead of the *Horatio* – a tribute to the key figure of our sea story

The 'Fortress built by Nature': an airman's view of the Needles and its famous lighthouse

all manner of invaders crossed the triumphant sea as though it were no moat at all – Romans; Angles, Saxons and Jutes; Danes and Normans; and, even after that, various pretenders to 'this royal throne of Kings'. There is not, in fact, any continuous awareness of the fort-like qualities of this island until the last of the old invaders – Henry VII – had successfully invaded. Then he, and still more, his famous son, by their very awareness saw to it that, in future, none should come uninvited. So, though the Britons in their coracles strove gallantly against the might of Rome; though Alfred, for a time, successfully met the Danes on their own element, and in drakars whose design he borrowed from theirs; though Hubert de Burgh with his clumsy round-ships, saved King John's England from the French in the grim battle off Dover, it was only Henry VIII who deliberately built the permanent 'wooden walls' for no other purpose but to keep the foreigner out. And so successful was he that all who followed caught on to the idea. Since his day, indeed, England has been invaded, but – successfully – only by insignificant forces slipping past the Navy, or else by virtue of that Navy, or some considerable part of it, welcoming the invader. More often, however, the intruder has been rudely thrown back: and, more often still, fatally discouraged from facing so bleak a venture, he has not even started.

Examples are many, from the days of King Harry himself, when the Most Catholic Kings of Europe would have given the brightest jewels in their crowns to make that arch-iconoclast smart: when Philip II sent his Invincible Armada against the detestable heretic Elizabeth – and paid for it with the bluest blood of Spain: when Louis XIV, *Grand Monarque*, wielder of vast armies, sought to gain that dominance of Europe which this insignificant island almost alone was thwarting: again and again during the eighteenth century, when France sought, by invasion, to get the lead into her own hand, and play her strong suit – her army – against our weakness: when in Napoleon's time, 'those storm-beaten ships, upon which the Grand Army never looked, stood between it and the dominion of the world': to the time, within living memory, when Wilhelm's Germany hoped to succeed where Napoleon had failed: and, nearer yet, when Hitler's and Goering's hopes, similar and just as sanguine, met with an identical fate.

But now we have reached the Air Age, and see, in the Battle of Britain and indeed throughout the Second World War, precisely the same strategic offensive on the part of our foes, the same strategic defence on our own: only, now, Hurricanes and Spitfires played their part along with Carriers, Battleships, Cruisers, Destroyers and Submarines, where before the brunt had fallen upon Cog, Great Ship, Galleon, Ship-of-the-Line and Battleship: bequeathing a galaxy of great and beloved names – *Grâce à Dieu, Revenge, Ark Ralegh, Sovereign of the Seas, Royal George, Victory, Iron Duke, Ark Royal*; all equally, from Coracle to Comet, defending and successfully defending

> 'This fortress, built by nature for herself
> Against infection and the hand of war.'

But defence is only half – even the lesser half – of the story. Evidently the history of Britain, and still more of the Commonwealth, is *not* the tale of a safety-first people sitting pretty behind the moat and walls of a purely defensive fortress. It may be well, this time, to begin with today and work backwards.

This island has lately been called an 'Unsinkable Aircraft Carrier': a *primary* offensive weapon, that is, of modern warfare, anchored close in with potentially hostile territory. This indeed is an image, in fact though perhaps not in fancy, to be set against Shakespeare's 'moat' and 'wall'. It enshrines, to quote our gallant neighbours, the *reculer pour mieux sauter* idea – the recoil to make the spring more effective. History, too, reveals the stark necessity for such a strategy: again and again it underlines this country's amiable, truly democratic, yet suicidally dangerous habit of being entirely unprepared for the final arbitrament of war. Does history perhaps reveal *why*, perennially, we indulge this apparently suicidal complex?

The basic reason, surely, is our steady refusal to regard war as the norm and peace as the exception. Our minds instinctively work in the opposite direction. In peace this Britain has been for centuries an indefatigable exporter, of commodities both material and spiritual. Over and above the purely material, she has exported, to name but a few, her virile sons and daughters, explorers, colonists, administrators, missionaries, business men, complete with distinctive tongue and very distinctive way of life, now to be traced in their millions to the uttermost ends of the earth. There are, too, the more institutional and ethical exports, commodities of world-acknowledged worth – her Parliamentary democracy; her particular brand of law; liberty of the individual; of worship, of speech, of the press; the Four Freedoms; hatred of wanton aggression, anywhere and everywhere; hatred of heresy-hunting, slavery and political oppression; sportsmanship – the knack of 'taking it' with a grin; Free Trade, fair competition, the freedom and safety of the seas. On balance, we may fairly claim that the good in the sum total of our exports has far outweighed the bad.

And another thing is incontestable. In putting all our energies into this enterprising and successful export-drive, we have forgotten, usually, that both enterprise and success are apt to invite envy, to breed enmity. Not once, but many times this unwelcome truth has suddenly been forced upon us: again and again we have realised it, almost too late.

Almost! Here is the point. Why not *quite*? The answer, of course, is the Moat: the Walls. They have coloured all our history: they have saved us time and again – that fluid Moat, those mobile Walls, behind which we can withdraw while this same enterprise of ours beats our ploughshares into swords, enabling us to sally forth again *when we are ready*. Examine dispassionately all our major wars from Marlborough's to Hitler's. Their common pattern is strikingly the same – first, reverses, monotonously regular on land, but often at sea too: then withdrawal – the 'defence phase', the 'recoil' of the proverb: next the waiting, preparative period, which we owe so entirely to the Moat and Walls; during which, let us not be so churlish as to forget, the sane, the freedom-loving peoples of the earth gather to our side, either within or without the Moat: and, last, the break-out, the offensive, when at length we can make our spring really effective – formerly by sea, but now by sea and air. What after all was D-Day but the greatest and truest combined offensive operation, by sea, by air, by land, that man has ever undertaken?

So much for the general pattern. But odd similarities keep cropping up in material detail too, even in such unlikely things as the ships themselves. It was in a tiny paddle-propelled coracle that the British fighter took the sea against that famous dictator, Caesar: it was in a rubber paddle-propelled float that his airborne descendant, two thousand years later, came back from fighting the more infamous Führer. How essentially alike they are! Again, consider the 'little ships' of Dunkirk, that episode often, though wrongly, labelled 'unique', 'miraculous'. Assuredly it is neither. Its basic characteristic is not its novelty, but its hoary antiquity. At almost any time before the Tudors, any sea-crisis, when it arose, was resolved precisely as Dunkirk was resolved – by a hurried assembly of 'little ships', owned and manned by a fortuitous collection of ordinary Englishmen, mostly seafarers, called to the danger-spot by a semi-organised 'embargo'. Indeed, before our modern fighting Navy came into being, there was no other force to

Ark Royal, 1588, the flagship of Queen Elizabeth's fleet which defeated the Armada, displacement 800 tons
Ark Royal, 1950, launched by Queen Elizabeth – Britain's newest aircraft carrier, displacement 36,800 tons

Nelson with his captains, the greatest of many great British admirals. *Below:* Douglas Bader, one of The Few

assemble. We must not run historical parallels to death, though. There were present, off and over Dunkirk, highly professional elements that would not have been there five centuries before – the R.N. and the R.A.F. – and no-one in his senses would underestimate *their* part.

All that had happened, of course, was that there had suddenly arisen an unpredictable crisis, with which for all their rich store of efficiency and experience, the regular services could not cope – it was physically impossible for either Navy or Air Force to evacuate the Army in such numbers. All that could be done – that was done, with a minimum of fuss – was to resurrect, at a moment's notice, the almost wholly forgotten machinery of mediaeval England, when, upon emergency, the King's officers went forth to the ports and creeks where his subjects' ships lay, requisitioned them then and there, and sent them off instantly to the danger-spot.

We are not a pugnacious people; not particularly history-conscious; not at all sentimental; not noticeably given to hero-worship. Yet by some queer, instinctive grasp of essentials, we do contrive to preserve, in a few outstandingly vivid vignettes, certain key-figures in our incomparable sea-story: Humphrey Gilbert, colonial pioneer, sitting, book in hand, in the stern of the *Squirrel* 'of burthen 10 tunnes', in the heart of the full Atlantic tempest which next moment engulfed him, quietly telling his comrades, 'We are as neere to Heaven by sea as by land': shrewd, stocky, merry-eyed little Drake, straightening himself, bowl in hand, to give his sublimely banal commentary on one of the great climacterics of England's life – 'They must wait their turn, good souls!'; or, having run out of powder, making up to the enemy with renewed fierceness, 'Being resolved', as he said, 'to put on a brag': Richard Grenville's dying defiance, ordering the Master Gunner to 'split and sink the ship': quiet, scholarly Blake, monumentally understating one of his more forceful offensive actions as 'keeping the foreigner from fooling us': blunt old cavalryman Monk, fighting his first naval action against the world's master-admiral, and astonishing his helmsmen by suddenly roaring, 'Right wheel! Charge!': Hawke, with coldly calculating fury, without pilots and in a gale, following the retreating enemy into a rock-strewn bay of which he had no chart: Nelson at Copenhagen, in the very heat of action playing that famous schoolboy prank with his telescope; and at Trafalgar, on the *Victory*'s musket-swept quarter deck, to his mortal hurt insisting on wearing the stars of his orders: Captain Oates, 'a very gallant gentleman', stumbling blindly out into the Antarctic night, and Scott quietly writing to the last as he awaited the inevitable end: Jellicoe, 'the only man who could lose the war in an afternoon', making with insufficient data, his copybook deployment at Jutland: Cunningham's instinctive flair for putting first things first when invited, at Crete, to leave the Army to its fate, 'It takes three years to build a cruiser, but three hundred to build a tradition.' Bader, crashing, with artificial legs bent beyond apparent repair, yet airborne again within half an hour, having got his artificer to re-bend them on the spot.

Whatever else they were, not one of these men could possibly be called 'defence-minded'. Yet there were moments in the lives of all of them when they had cause to bless the Moat. It is, indeed, the subtle combination of the Moat, the Walls, and individuals like these which has enabled us to survive – and to prosper.

But, to end just where we started, history, regarded as a collection of facts in the past tense, does not repeat itself. Perish the thought! There lies complacency, there lurks potential disaster.

Yesterday can never be today. In many respects, indeed, tomorrow looks unpleasantly unlike yesterday. The Moat, already, is a deal more shrunken, far more leapable; Walls – even today, and how much more tomorrow – must be of more complex texture than wood or steel if they are to be still 'defensive to a house'. They must have wings, for instance; they must have the magical eyes and ears which modern science can give them. Since too, a single atom bomb on London could take more lives in a minute than the whole of the Luftwaffe took in five years of frantic endeavour, commonsense dictates that the time between the 'recoil' and the 'spring' be reduced to the barest minimum. And this is true, not only for us but for all that free world which, yesterday, drew to our side, and – who can doubt it? – tomorrow would do the same; as surely, in spirit, it always must.

2
LANDSCAPE WITH FIGURES

By L.A.G. Strong

Any attempt to find consistency in the British scene or the British character must fail from the start, not only because both offer a variety which no other country of the same size can compass, but because the characteristics which make up that variety vary in themselves from day to day. Yet the British character is everywhere recognised. It stands for something constant. And the British scene – anyone from another country will at once pick out features which to his mind represent it and no other. In fact, we and the land we live in make up an intractable and energetic paradox.

A consistent line of approach may seem to yield results at first; but the pleasure will not last long. Ah, says the investigator, Britain is a complex of different races. Let us adopt the ethnological approach, and study, not the people, but the peoples of Britain. Happening upon a Surrey village, he discovers to his joy a cluster of Danish surnames, half the owners of which show Scandinavian build and colouring. He makes splendid headway with these, explaining away the physical variants by intermarriage, and has great fun in postulating the original Danish settlement of which they are the results – until he finds that only one family has been in the place for more than a generation, and the rest have come at different times from all over the country, can give no ethnological reason for being where they are, and are profoundly uninterested in the whole enquiry.

One blond Viking (who managed to be more rustically English than anyone in the village) was asked whether he minded his daughter marrying a Canadian. He looked puzzled. Then his face cleared.

'No-o-o,' he pronounced slowly. 'Why for? 'Tis good stock.'

Baffled in Surrey, the investigator goes, let us say, to Devon and Cornwall, in search of Celts and what not. Here he has better luck. True, the discovery of whole tribes of people called

Right: Runnymede, calm, almost sleepy scene of a most stormy meeting ... and on the river, swans

Moses who have no connection with Jewry throws him out of his stride; but there is a wealth of swarthy persons, he hears tales which he can well believe of Spanish strains dating from the survivors of the Armada, he finds French words in the Devon dialect, plus some pure Chaucer, and he can spend as long as he likes poring over Cornish place names and such stimulating surnames as Eva, Poad, Treweek, Treguddick, and Bosustow. He reads near St. Austell a notice pinned on a gate: 'The man what belongs stealing turnips out of this field, better watch out for the police.' Taking tea at Sheepstor, he hears a girl scold a refractory kitten and shut it in a coal cellar, with the injunction that it is 'entitled to bide there till the company is went.' He observes with stupefaction that Dartmoor Prison has been taken as a model by certain local architects, and that houses are to be seen for miles round which reproduce faithfully in miniature its most intimidating features.

In Devon he finds at least three dialects, of which the chief point of likeness is that they happily overturn the normal English treatment of pronouns: 'Us'll go along o' she if her'll come along o' we.' In Yorkshire he finds five or six, those of the North and West Riding resembling each other so little that each denies the other's right to be called Yorkshire at all. He learns that speech in England varies so much that a Bradford mill-owner can tell from what part of the town, sometimes even from what street his workers come; and that a lady wrote to the famous broadcaster Freddie Grisewood, after one of his 'Our Bill' sketches, saying, 'You come either from A or B' – two Oxfordshire villages – and he came from A.

It is only when the visitor gives up all hope of consistent results, and settles down to enjoy the mad diversity of Britain, that he begins to get the total feeling, the atmosphere, the character which that diversity creates. He goes to Windsor, to the stately heart of England. On the Fourth of June he visits Eton – 'What

Right: Features that represent the British scene: carvings on the Downs, like the White Horse of Westbury
Below: 'The investigator goes to Devon and Cornwall in search of Celts and what not': Looe harbour

do you call this?' an American officer enquired, staring at the boys in their toppers and tails. 'An OCTU for undertakers?' – and sees one of the few survivals of an England gracious, unhurried, untroubled, of a life that still goes on as though unaware that the sanctions for it, the assumptions on which its ceremonial is based, have gone for ever. As though unaware; in fact, Eton is very much aware, strangely alert to the world about it; but it is one of our British habits to keep a ritual, and the ritual of the Fourth of June, the circulating crowds, the band, the cricket on Agar's Plough, can still grip friend and stranger alike. As for the fireworks afterwards, and the Procession of Boats, when boat after boat comes from darkness into glare, and the crews stand precariously, holding up their oars, and pass before the crowd, to disappear like ghosts into the murk, with the light still gleaming on the wet uplifted oar blades: one need not be very imaginative to see in the scene a symbol of youth today, a new meaning given to an ancient rite – and, anyway, the scene is strange and beautiful and not to be forgotten.

Then, close to Eton, Runnymede, the calm and almost sleepy scene of a most stormy meeting which laid one of England's foundation stones; and, on the river, swans, figures in almost every English landscape which has water in it. You will see them on our lakes, in our rivers, our tidal waters, sometimes even in the sea: and, of course, at Stratford, where presumably they have always been, so that the title 'Swan of Avon' came naturally to hand for Stratford's First Citizen.

Travelling around, while summer is still with him, the visitor comes perhaps to Wales, looking first at the mountains. They are harder to see in winter: though, if one of the rare clear winter days can be found, there can be no lovelier encounter with them than to drive, say, from Bangor to Capel Curig, wander around while the sun is up, and then return through the terrifying pass, where towering stone and darkness seem one and the same. The mountain people, the shepherds and farmers, are courteous, reserved, and charming, like mountain people almost everywhere. They will show you a ewe that lived ten days buried in a snowdrift, and seemed unperturbed when at last they dug her out. They will point out the rocks where, every year, students and visitors fall to death because they will not believe in the danger. Indeed, safety first is a motto well known in these parts. One local taxi conveyed an admiring visitor at a steady eight to ten miles an hour, on the crown of the road. Just as he was about to remark on it, the driver spoke.

'Effery one is drifing fery fasst nowadayss. Twice I haf peen run into from pehind.'

Another taxi driver, on the coast, picked up a party stranded at the station, and drove them to their hotel three miles out. They made a full load, and a girl sat with the driver.

'Look you,' he was saying presently, 'I want you to do a thing for me now. Do you see that island, right out beyont there? Well now, I want you to go for me, at sunset now, any fine night, right down as near as you can to that island, and you will hear all the seals barking before they go to sleep.'

One such island, at Cardigan, is said to be one of the few homes left to the gray seal. Certainly gray seals abound there. They are very tame, and will rise close inshore to stare with mild and attentive wonder at the visitor – especially if he sing or whistle softly. There are seals off Cornwall too. They sport in the rough seas at Tintagel; a baby seal, barely three feet long, came and gambolled beside me one summer day at Sennen: but nowhere have I seen so many as off the West Highlands, where, in October, as we rowed into the Sound of Arisaig with my wife playing soft major chords on a small accordion, at one time we counted forty swimming heads in the clear, pearly water behind us.

Many of the British seaside resorts are best seen in winter. Brighton, magnificent, genial, vulgar, aristocratic (with its beautiful Regency houses, rivalling those of Bristol and Bath), laid out to amuse the visitor, and with an air so bracing that one is hungry after a

Right: Sometimes fog can unexpectedly turn a commonplace landscape into an exquisite Japanese print

couple of hours inside its boundaries – Brighton is at its best in the winter months. So, despite East winds, are some of the Norfolk towns, and the cluster of coast towns around Newcastle-on-Tyne.

The cathedral cities need autumn or spring. Wet light, sunshine after rain, transfigures Oxford, Winchester, Gloucester, York, and those noble and gracious ruins of which Fountains is by common consent the loveliest. A bus ride to Fountains from Harrogate provided an instance of the local character, the driver proving well-informed, interested, and humorous, with one of those splendid Yorkshire voices, warm, deep, and resonant, which have made J. B. Priestley a front-rank broadcaster and given Huddersfield perhaps the most famous choir in England. A character? Yes, but a genuine character: not a character turn.

These characters you will find everywhere. Their quality is difficult to reproduce. On paper, what was spontaneous often sounds studied and artificial. The vicar of a parish in a Lancashire industrial town told me a short dialogue which he vowed he had not touched up. Wandering in the country some miles from home, he came to a village churchyard. The sexton, an old man, was slowly digging a grave. He took no notice at all of the visitor, who, with a townsman's garrulity, tried to get into conversation with him.

VICAR: Good afternoon. It's very quiet down here.
SEXTON: (jerking his thumb downwards) Quieter down theer.
VICAR: Do you bury them often here?
SEXTON: Only once.
VICAR: (a last attempt) Have you been doing this all your life?
SEXTON: Not yet.

Evidently Hamlet's gravedigger was drawn from life.

A Devonshire farmer of my acquaintance used to drive an astonishing old pony and trap,

'Travelling around while summer is still with him'. In the Cotswolds

the pony fat and lethargic, the trap like a coffin on wheels. Its pace was funereal, yet he always arrived dead on time, no matter what the distance. I asked him how he managed it. His brow furrowed.

'Well, you see, 'tis like this here. I says to myself, when 'ave I got to be there? Such and such a hour. Vurry gude. Next I says, what's the time now? Such and such a time. Vurry gude. Then I makes a calculation, and I drives accordin' to.'

Character at its sharpest, its swiftest, is to be enjoyed in the mother city. Even though the traditional occupations of bus driver and bargee have lost some of their richness by the incursion of petrol and the relative obscuring of canal traffic, the Cockney still keeps his quickness of repartee and his gift of summing up a situation in a phrase. Again, in most cases the characteristic is not the words themselves, but in their fitness as part of an occasion and the way in which they crystallize its quality and, if it is an unhappy occasion, take the sting from it.

On one of the worst nights of the blitz, a group of about thirty people was huddled into a small mews shelter near Earls Court. The air was foul, but the continuous crashing outside made escape worse than foolhardy. Sleep was impossible. Slowly, steadily, the shelterers' spirits sank, headaches and cramp grew worse, till by about four in the morning every one felt round about zero. Then a Cockney voice cut through the gloom.

'Coo,' it observed. 'My morale ain't 'alf . . . . low!'

The blank had been powerfully filled; for a moment there was silence. Then everybody laughed – and at once tension was eased, depression gone, and a new life breathed in the place.

An old gentleman, finding a long queue at a London terminus, wisely walked out into the street to look for a taxi there. A small boy,

An aerial photograph of the Llangynog Valley, Montgomeryshire, one of the loveliest valleys in Wales

seeing him, undertook to call one, whistled catastrophically, attracting the attention of half the street, and secured a taxi. As it drew up, and he made for the door, a bigger boy shoved him aside, and held the door open. The small boy exclaimed indignantly.

'Come orf it,' he cried. 'I seen the old basket first – didn' I, Sir?'

The Cockney excels, too, at those dark sayings which one is sometimes lucky enough to catch in passing, but can never complete, can never imagine what led up to them, or what could follow.

One night, when thick fog shrouded the Waterloo Road, two women in shawls and cloth caps made sinister shapes in the gloom. One was addressing the other in a hoarse, thick whisper.

'If I'd a known then,' she confided, 'wot I knows nah, I'd never 'ave weaned 'im!'

It is a colourful neighbourhood, that stretches from Waterloo Road to Blackfriars on the one side and Walworth and Camberwell on the other. One of its Sunday morning sights was a retired boxer, an ex-world-champion, offering to guess the weight of any bystander. If he came within two pounds of it, you gave him a penny. If not, he got nothing. His method of appraisal was an up and down look and a grasp on one's biceps: and four times out of five he drew his money.

To a district like this fog makes less difference than to most, especially when the street markets are on. Naphtha flares come as near as most things to beating fog, and the people, being intensely gregarious and seldom moving far afield, have little occasion to get lost. Indeed, with our national knack of turning misfortunes to advantage, we sometimes score unexpectedly from fog. It can dignify our meanest architecture, or turn a commonplace suburban or village scene into an exquisite Japanese print. Admittedly, along some of our by-passes and arterial roads we could do with fog all the time: but this is one of the many ways in which the figures have defaced the landscape. They do not mean to deface it. They go about their purposes, and defacement

The face under the pointed hat is full of life and character and the dress serves only to set it off

results. Sometimes, in their lust for whatever it is they want, they produce – with the help of the English climate – an incongruous beauty. In certain lights, the vast slag heaps, the conical tips and refuse dumps can take on a mellow dignity of their own. There has been too little planning in this sense, too little care of what we have, too much freedom for the vandal to exploit the land. Stonehenge is robbed of privacy by graceless encroachments from another age. What Wordsworth called

'The grassy barrows of the happier dead'

have here and there been removed to make a level space for army manoeuvres. There is no bestiality to which the official mind will not incline unless powers exist to stop it, and stop it promptly. Yes: sometimes the landscape would be happier without the figures.

It is when figures and landscape are in harmony that Britain shows at her best. In the

Left: The old folk have a strength of individuality which no degree of mechanisation can remove

Cotswolds, the buildings harmonise with the landscape because the men who built them understood it and were themselves a part of it. The people who best show this harmony, the interdependence of people and places are, naturally enough, the old, who have had time to be moulded and marked by the place where they have spent their lives. Sitting at cottage doors, ambling along to church on Sunday morning, gossiping in almshouses, the old folk of Britain have a strength of individuality which no degree of mechanisation can remove. In the almshouses, perhaps, they are given a specious individuality by the uniforms of a bygone time: but the face underneath the pointed hat or the peaked cap is full of life and character, and the dress serves only to set it off.

Incidentally, these old almshouses are often among the loveliest examples of architecture in the country. You will find them in all sorts of unexpected places, large and small. Those at Abingdon, for instance, and the Lord Leycester Hospital at Warwick, deserve all the admiration they are given: and much of the charm of so many almshouses comes from their unexpectedness, the way in which they are tucked away in the most unlikely places.

The Kent country, with its oasthouses and its hopfields, has a character and a beauty which mark it off sharply from every other district: qualities as distinctive as the great rolled barrier of the Sussex Downs, seen at their best between Lewes and Lancing, and the wooded hangers of Petersfield and Harting.

The Lake District deserves a chapter to itself. It again, on the rare days when rain is not drawing curtains across the mountains, has a winter beauty which suits it even better than its luxuriant summers; a clarity, an articulation of line which summer blurs. Not everyone appreciates its beauties. During the war a number of Cockneys were evacuated to Keswick. They made no secret of their disapproval.

'At any rate,' protested a Keswick lady to a matron from the Elephant and Castle, 'you must admit that our mountains are beautiful.'

'Wot!' exclaimed the matron. 'Them bloody 'umps?'

Geologists are happy in the Lake District, and in many far less spectacular. The coast above Bridlington delights them, with two totally dissimilar strata disputing for supremacy on the cliffs and rocks. They are excited by the many-coloured sands of Alum Bay, in the Isle of Wight. The Island is a microcosm with a quite astonishing variety; yet another landscape best seen in autumn or in winter, if its full beauty of line and colour is to sink into the visitor's perceptions.

There are people to whom Walberswick and other spots on the Suffolk coast are the best in the whole of Britain. Lovers of the Norfolk Broads will go nowhere else for their holiday. No one who has seen their autumn colouring will forget the woods above Chepstow, nor those between Savernake and Marlborough. In June, the patches of viper's bugloss beside the road between Blandford and Salisbury make one wonder if this is England at all. But why go on cataloguing sights and memories? We end up where we started. The English landscape is as varied as the English character, and each is a part of the other.

Right: Shaftesbury in Dorset, looking down Gold Hill to Blackmore Vale, in the Thomas Hardy country

3
THE ENGLISH SCENE

By Osbert Lancaster

Above all else the English scene is artificial. No race has talked about Nature or drawn inspiration from her to the extent that we have, and nowhere in the world is she kept more firmly under control than in England. Our landscape, of which we are justly proud, is a work of art in the exact meaning of the term: save in a few isolated pockets in the Fells or on Dartmoor, no acre of the English countryside is, nor has been for centuries, in anything that approaches a natural state. In the south, with its long lines of globular elms and thickset hedgerows, the countryside as it appears today is the handiwork of eighteenth-century planners and theorists. In the east, where the primaeval wastes of reeds and mudflats have been drained and channelled, it has been formed by seventeenth-century hydraulic engineers. In the lowlands everywhere, countless generations of agriculturalists from the early Bronze Age onward have been sweeping away all traces of the swamp and forest.

The role of architect and town planner here has, therefore, for a long time, at least since the seventeenth century, been subtly different from that of his colleagues abroad. The relation between architecture and landscape is far closer and more complicated where the latter can be made to conform to the prevailing taste almost as easily as bricks and mortar. What could be brought about elsewhere only in very specialized conditions, such as those prevailing in the France of Louis Quatorze or the Italy of the Neapolitan Bourbons, was commonplace here from at least 1700 onwards. Half the country estates of England are the expression of an aesthetic conception less grandiose though infinitely subtler than that which inspired *le Grand Monarque*, but every bit as artificial.

But this influence was mutual; not only did the canons of architectural taste materially alter the appearance of the landscape, but the character of the landscape insensibly affected the canons of architectural taste. And this it is which gives to English architecture its unique quality. Versailles and Caserta spread the influence of their pompous formality over

Left: Countless generations have made the English landscape a work of art in the exact meaning of the term

Chatsworth House, home of the Dukes of Devonshire, and one of the stateliest of English country houses

hundreds of acres of the surrounding countryside; but in the country houses of England, with certain notable exceptions (such as Blenheim and Seaton Delaval, which, noble works as they are, retain a faint exoticism that is understandable in a Leoni but puzzling in a Vanbrugh), the formality has been softened, the pediments and porticoes rendered less rigid, and the fluttering and writhing of the draperies pendant from the statues along the balustrade are stirred by a more tempered, less violent, wind than that which blows down the long colonnades of the high Baroque: for thanks to the modifying influence of the landscape, the grand gesture, the theatrical sweep, are here made to appear, ever so faintly, absurd.

Marked as is the influence of this ingrained empiricism in the countryside, its effects, sometimes disastrously so, are even more obvious in our towns. Here, to the modifying circumstances of nature are added those hardly less powerful of usage and tradition. Save in a very few isolated instances – Bath is one – the rational plan has always been anathema, and convenience is always subordinated to individual idiosyncrasy or an almost superstitious conservatism. It is this trait in the national character that gives rise both to *les grandeurs et les misères* of the contemporary urban scene, and which, when recognised and consciously exploited, results in the aesthetic of the picturesque. No sooner does some enthusiast, fresh from a visit to more logical lands, lay out an elegant piazza or cut some triumphal processional way than its classical perfection is promptly wrecked by installing a fruit market or an opera house, or both, on the same site, or by obstinately retaining, just where some great monumental structure is necessary to close the carefully planned vista, a pickle factory.

It is this refusal to follow the logical course

Knole, with its seven courtyards, twelve staircases, and a room for every day of the year, covers five acres

which gives to our cities, and to London in particular, their great visual quality of unexpectedness and it is a quality which the greatest of our architects have perfectly understood and appreciated. Thus Wren, despite a half-hearted effort to sell the Government a careful plan on the continental model for the surroundings of St. Paul's (a plan, incidentally, which anyone who takes the trouble to study it alongside a contour map can see at a glance would never have worked), realised finally that the dramatic effect of his great dome would be immeasurably heightened by its sudden revelation above the tops of the surrounding brick terraces, or by being seen filling the entire sky at the end of some narrow alley. (The ghastly mistake which subsequent generations have made has been to allow the surrounding buildings to encroach not horizontally but vertically, and, moreover, abandoning in their construction London stock brick in favour of stone and concrete, thus for ever destroying that wonderful contrast between the high gleaming mass of white Portland stone and the rich dark brown of the low houses alongside. And this is a mistake which no number of ornamental gardens or open vistas will rectify).

A third factor of which those responsible for the English scene have been ever mindful is the weather. In our climate the actual appearance of a building, in so far as this depends on the texture, which is far more than is often realised, changes immensely rapidly and it is not sufficient for an architect simply to have a clear idea of what his building will look like at the moment of completion, but also of its appearance after a few winters of sleet and fog and soot. If he is too simple his noble conception will soon look impossibly sordid and battered; if he is too clever, and

A famous example of piecemeal planning. The Strand as it looked in 1900, before a section of it was widened

takes steps to preserve its first bright gleam — as various new materials and methods of construction now render perfectly feasible — the result will be even worse for his creation will forever appear to be the one false tooth in an otherwise natural denture.

The danger which constantly threatens the English scene today arises not nearly so much from carelessness as from sentimentality combined with a passion for uniformity. That passion for having things in keeping results on the one hand in having power-stations dolled up to look like Border castles (or rather used to, for latterly this has been the lesser menace), and on the other in pulling down some perfectly inoffensive, and indeed often impressive, early nineteenth-century warehouse, because it is thought to conflict with the arty-crafty little housing estate, or not very distinguished seventeenth-century manor-house in the foreground. The classic example of this particular manifestation of the rage for improvement is the periodic demand for the removal of the railway bridge above Ludgate Hill. So far from detracting from the effect of St. Paul's as seen from Fleet Street, it immensely adds to it; rising above the smoke of the passing trains which are rendered toy-like by its enormous silhouette in the background, the great dome takes on a majesty and a significance which would at once vanish were the bridge removed.

These structures hold equally good in the domestic sphere. The half-dozen or so surviving untouched Adam interiors, complete with all their original furnishings and hung with contemporary paintings, are great works of art, and long may they be preserved. But they can be paralleled elsewhere, and it is not in them that the visitor will discover the

The graceful achievement of an eighteenth-century town plan. Harmony and elegance in Royal Crescent, Bath

peculiar national quality of the English scene which renders it unique. It is likely to be far more strongly evident in those houses where every generation has left its mark and a single-minded preoccupation with 'period' perfection has not been allowed to steam-roller the past: where the repellent features of the first Earl inexpertly limned by an anonymous Elizabethan hack are found alongside the sixth Countess, in an enormous bustle and chignon, by G. F. Watts: where the Regency ballroom is entered from a Jacobean hall and leads to what was an eighteenth-century library until it was given a Morris wallpaper at the end of the last century; where the panelling is Queen Anne, the water-colours Victorian, and the furniture of the comfortable but unobtrusive kind generally known as 'club'.

A sense of the past is among the most valuable, and the most dangerous of our national characteristics. On the one hand it encourages us to leave well alone, to pay due respect to our fathers and to allow time and weather to do their work; on the other, it leads us too frequently into equating age with value and to see merit where in fact there is only antiquity. Thus we fall into the error of assuming the older automatically to be the better and of sacrificing the Georgian east wing in order to get a better view of the mediaeval Great Hall, or substituting bogus modern stained glass windows in place of Victorian under the mistaken impression that they accord better with the Perpendicular tracery. At its worst it leads to the nailing of strips of deal across perfectly inoffensive Greek façades in order to give that half-timbered Jacobethean air which for some reason is now thought to be *de rigueur* for all inns and country hotels, and which achieved what was certainly

Below: King's College Chapel, Cambridge, outstanding example of late Perpendicular splendour. *Right*: St. Mary's, Oxford; an unexpected combination of Perpendicular window tracery with a Baroque porch

the most fantastic, and one hopes the ultimate, expression of hay-wire antiquarianism in the half-timbered buffet cars of British Railways.

Given time, a certain basic good sense, and a careful choice of materials, almost any building will take its place in the English scene and in due course make its own peculiar contribution to the whole. The academic façades and symmetrical lay-out of eighteenth-century squares and terraces which must at the time of their erection have appeared embarrassingly chilly and formal have long since taken their honoured place in the ensemble. The neo-Gothic rectories and barge-boarded villas of the mid-Victorian era now give rise to little unfavourable comment. Even the factories and the warehouses, however disastrous their impact may have been socially, from the aesthetic point of view have attained a certain value. It is only those buildings in which use has been made of such unattractive materials as glazed bricks, or in which the architect abandoned all good sense in a striving for originality or, and these are the most numerous, buildings which are inspired by a self-conscious good taste, where the effort to 'be in keeping' is imperfectly concealed, which will for ever strike a discordant note.

It is this mixture of weathered formality and sudden surprise which gives to the English scene its peculiar quality and which sets it apart from other landscapes, and it is just this combination which the planners and the preservation boys are doing their best to destroy. One can savour it in individual buildings – St. Mary's Church at Oxford for instance, with its fantastic Baroque porch and Perpendicular window tracery – and time and again in the works of the painters. The fantastic, stepped, spire of St. George's, Bloomsbury rising above the squalor and ruination of Hogarth's Gin Lane; that strange hexagonal shot-tower which impinges so frequently on the foreground of Canaletto's river scenes; the innumerable advertisements for gin and blacking which cover the walls of Cruickshank's courts and alleys; all these give hints and pointers towards the isolation of something which must always remain in the last analysis indefinable.

In other capitals the landscape effects are immediate and two-dimensional; once seen, the great vista of the *Champs Elysées* will not alter or expand however far one walks along it, for it contains no surprises; so dominant is the dome of St. Peter's that one can never forget its existence and its every appearance on the Roman scene has a quality of inevitability.

But in London, as one walks along the Embankment, the relationships of church spires and warehouses, office blocks and breweries is ever changing, the contrasts ever new, and each time one sees across some blitzed basement or sandwiched between the arches of a viaduct, or rising above a tattered hoarding, the vast bulk of St. Paul's, one sees it, once more, for the first time.

Left : St. Paul's, rising above the smoke of passing trains – rendered toy-like by its towering dome

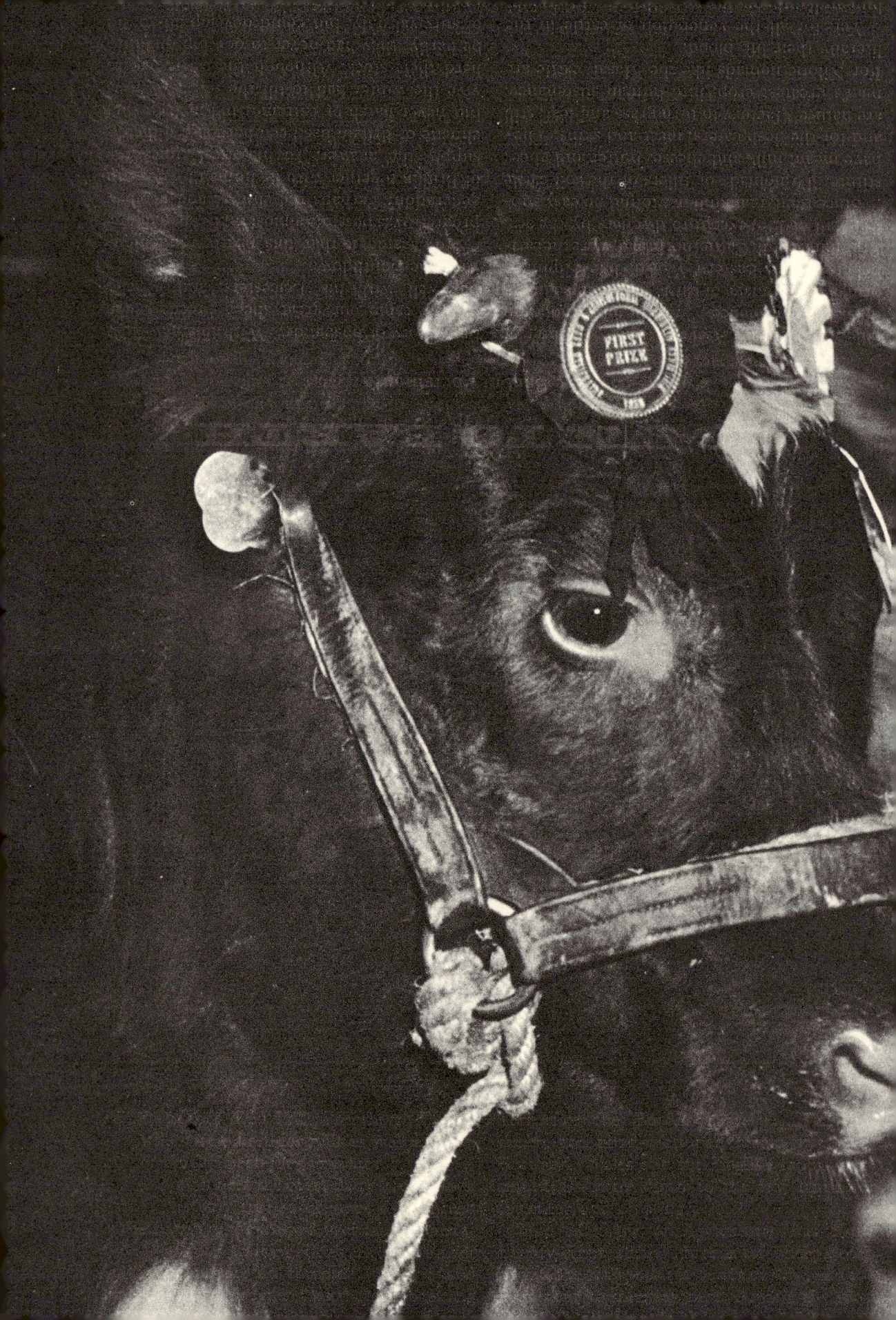

4
DOWN TO EARTH

By The Earl of Portsmouth

'Oiled and curled Assyrian bulls smelling of musk and insolence . . .' The old quotation brings up an image of cattle sacred in so many beliefs of the Eastern World, like Kipling's Brahminee bull. Cattle, not bread, were the earliest staff of life, except to dwellers by the sea.

Since then, mankind has found no easy substitute. To nomads or tillers of the soil cattle have meant milk and cheese, butter and ghee; and for the flesh eaters, meat and skins. They are nature's factory to turn grass and leaf, still man's greatest crop, into human sustenance. For Nilotic nomads like the Masai, cattle are literally their life blood.

Yet, for all the veneration of cattle in the human Pantheon, it was in Britain of the eighteenth century that the greatest recorded strides in breed improvement have taken place. The great bulls like 'Comet' and 'Favourite' are symbols even now to every breeder. Men like the Collings brothers, Bates, and Booth are household words to the stock farmer. In the same way Coke of Norfolk and 'Turnip' Townsend are monumental figures in the history of husbandry. With this new husbandry came our great sheep breeders like Bakewell with his Leicesters, and Ellman with the Southdown.

How came it that this nearly miraculous progress was possible almost in the span of one generation? Perhaps the climate and geology of Britain together with its human breeds can supply the answer. In historical times the climate of Britain has been hard and difficult, but never harsh or extreme, and men to survive the winter had to till the soil as well as herd their stock. Although the cattle had to be hardy, they had never to develop qualities of survival only, but could develop all-round qualities, not sacrificing one function at the expense of another. They did not have to learn to go without water for days, or grow humps like the cattle of Asia and Africa with which to survive the bitter months of scarcity.

Secondly, the geology of Britain is such that there is no really poor soil, and it is so varied that it made for a multiplicity of individual types. Yet for all this early geographic isola-

Left: The young beef of Old England – the King's champion Shorthorn steer, 'Windsor Augusta'

Shorthorn sires like 'Comet', bred by Charles Collings, are household words still to every stock farmer

tion, the variation of our land field by field allowed cattle and sheep to develop complementary qualities so they could survive well in the poor harsh uplands and flourish in the rich fat vales.

Indeed, Britain is criss-crossed by green droving roads, some of them prehistoric, like Icknield Street across the Berkshire Downs. For the regular movement of stock developed from the earliest times.

Last, the people themselves were of a quality to use the gifts with which nature had endowed our Island. They had to be sturdy and independent to survive, and they had to be neatherd, shepherd, swineherd and farmer combined. From Celt came power to persist and clan organisation; from Anglo-Saxon, individuality and local order; from Dane, the spirit of commercial adventure and from Norman, administrative synthesis.

Until the nineteenth century the country was never overcrowded. All this meant that there was room for all who would work. Stock were not lean and stunted from over-grazing, the land was not over-cropped. In other words, the land never grew old and tired, nor did the hills become eroded spines of rock. While for agriculture itself soil and environment were ready to respond. Thus the foundations laid for stock were inherently good. Indeed it is not hard to believe that the cattle and sheep of the Middle Ages which had to provide traction, food, and clothing were sounder than the bad stock on the more indifferent farm of today.

With the opening of the New World and for better or worse, the great commercial stirring at the Reformation, leaders of agriculture in the country began to adumbrate the great upsurge of husbandry for crop and stock which

Long before Mendel's researches, the Collings brothers had made miraculous progress in selective breeding

reached its zenith at the end of the eighteenth century – an upsurge stimulated by the needs of a new and seething industrial population. As so often in our history the need found the men to answer it. Among our cattle the great breeds took shape, for it was then that the roast beef of Old England' became the desire of the people as well as the somewhat gouty privilege of the richer classes.

Long before Mendel's exact genetic researches, the Collings brothers with empiric artistry perfected certain beef qualities of the Teesdale Shorthorn, a work already begun by the Earls and Dukes of Northumberland. Milk and milk products too were needed, so their successors Booth on one side bred Shorthorns for the butcher; and Bates bred them for the pail.

Scotland (*pace* overseas and English enthusiasts) produced and still produces, the finest beef in the world. This is not a little due to the work of Amos Cruickshank of Sittyton, whose Shorthorns went abroad to sire the frozen meat of later days, and to the protagonists of the Aberdeen Angus and other good Northern breeds.

In England the Longhorn was developed for a transient period. Coke of Norfolk's tenant, John Reeve, evolved the Red Poll. On the Welsh Marches the Hereford came into its own, soon to be spread across the world. The Duke of Bedford and Coke of Norfolk encouraged the sweet Red Devon breed, still the favourite of many farmers in East Anglia for winter fattening. Other cattle, Lincoln Red, Welsh Black, Gloucesters, South Devon, Sussex and Galloways were improved, and continued as great standbys in their district, but never quite achieved the world-wide fame of Shorthorn, Angus, Hereford and Red Poll in the pedigree export market. Red Poll, Shorthorn, Devon and others were bred for milk as well as beef, but originally beef predominated.

Hotfoot on beef the great dairy breeds took shape; the only true indigenous dairy breed is the Ayrshire, developed over many generations for good milking qualities, fair butter fat, independence in foraging, stamina and longevity. Ayrshire men took the lead in testing for tuberculosis and recording yields of milk and butterfat.

It was the Channel Islands which produced the close-bred high-butterfat dairy breeds that have spread to become part of the main Island's stock. From Friesland, owing to our close intercourse with the Dutch in the seventeenth century and later, came the heaviest milking breed of all, the British Friesian, the Holstein of the New World.

Concurrently the British breeds of sheep as we now know them took shape. England's original rise in international commerce was based on wool. The Perpendicular period of English architecture – churches, early country houses and late castles – arose from the wealth of the wool and cloth trade. And this was the new wealth of England which gave the Tudors, miser or spendthrift, their flying start. The sheep were the long-woolled breeds, which then gave milk and fine cheese, but indifferent mutton. (Even up to 1939 some ewe's-milk cheese was made in Wales).

As the population grew, mutton as well as beef was needed, and so the old wool breeds evolved for dual purpose; the Southdown, a mutton sheep *par excellence*, with fine wool not quite rivalling the Merino, was the prototype of the short-wool Down breeds such as Hampshire Down, Suffolk, Oxford, Shropshire and Dorset. These became part and parcel of the new Norfolk arable system. Even in mediaeval days sheep were kept for fertility as much as wool. Now they became the golden hoof which fertilised and consolidated the new fields of turnip and aftermath of clover.

Robert Bakewell was probably the greatest of all the eighteenth-century breeders. To him we owe the long-woolled Leicester and its derivative the Border Leicester. The hill sheep, the good-muttoned long-wools from Scotland, Wales and the English moors continued to come down to the low lands for fattening and crossing.

The Ministry of Agriculture has listed twenty-eight British breeds of sheep, each adapted to its special style of country, and too numerous to mention here. Among the most famous is the Romney Marsh, useful in many countries, because, like the Irishman's bird, it had to be in two places at once. In summer it could live on the fat marshes, but in winter it had to move to the uplands of Kent and further afield. Again, the Clun is one of the most popular of modern sheep. This breed, like the Kerry Hill, derived from a cross between the long-woolled and the Down breeds, to become fixed in type. Classified as a short-wool, they yet have some of the virtues of both breeds.

Now, sheep and cattle owed most to the yeoman farmer, and husbandry to the great improving landowner. But pigs were improved by the genius in cottage and croft. To name but one example, the Yorkshire Large White, that father of the Occidental breakfast table, was brought to perfection by Joseph Tuley and his fellow Yorkshire weavers. As the whippet and the fighting cock were to the English miner, the pig was to his cottage forebears.

It was the eighteenth-century genius with animal and tillage that has made modern farming and the livestock breeds mentioned above. In six years 'Turnip' Townsend accomplished his astonishing revolution. His even more famous contemporary, who was both neighbour and rival, Coke of Norfolk, turned the sandy waste lands of Norfolk into ordered fertile fields, while the Dukes of Bedford drained fens which are still some of the richest lands in England.

At the same time, agricultural invention in machines began – not least Jethro Tull's corn drill, and indeed many mechanised wonders of today had their origins well over one hundred years ago.

Through the ordered centuries British farming has written its own history, which,

Above: 'The golden hoof and the aftermath of clover' ... A flock of ewes from Maiden Castle, in Dorset
Below: Sheep owed most to the farmer, cattle to the landowner, pigs to the genius of men in croft and cottage

41

read aright, has been the history of all her people. There have been economic recessions – the last one based on false economics endured to all intents and purposes from 1878 to 1939. But in spite of economics there has never been a true recession in the progress of farming knowledge and technique. For, however bitter the slump or the political changes, outstanding individuals have met the challenge and added something worth learning in the pioneer world of method or the knowledge of natural possibilities.

Today we are fighting animal and plant disease as never before. Our herds are persistently being cleared of such diseases as tuberculosis and epizootic abortion. Perhaps most important of all we are just beginning to learn that diseases may be checked, but not cured, by serum, drugs and sprays; in fact that the right conditions of environment and the study of inherent health (co-operation with nature) are the true lasting contribution to medicine and biologic progress. Quantity with disease is less vital than quality with health. But we may look forward to the time when yields of crop and stock may be maintained and even improved while disease and subnormality are reduced. It is doubtful if our younger farmers have ever been so alive and humble to learn as now.

Already the production of our narrowing acres compares favourably in proportion to the magnitude of our effort with that of any country in the world. For those who like such evidence, our fields are the most highly mechanised in the world. There is perhaps no country in the world where more has been and is being spent in proportion on the buildings and permanent equipment of its farms. At the same time, our husbandry is constantly essaying fresh methods, new crops, and improved varieties.

The work on grassland of Sir George Stapledon and his able team in our own times has made him fit to rank with the eighteenth-century giants. Were they all alive today, it would be impossible to name more fitting recipients of the Nobel Prize than Townsend and Coke, Bakewell and the Collings brothers, and last but by no means least, Stapledon, for better husbandry is the father of peace. And yet none of this would have been possible then, any more than now, without the stockman and tiller of the field.

Britain has produced on her soil a human richness of character, a slow sardonic wit, a sense of responsibility and duty to land and stock. British farm workers have kept a feeling for the essential order of nature as deep as that of their colleagues in any other country of the world.

When the writer first started farming he learnt more from his old ploughman, shepherd, and cowman than any books or university could tell him. Truth and justice, religion, and that piety which understands nature and fulfils its obligations to the land, is there in a measure not easily found elsewhere. Hard work and hard times have never robbed them of serenity, or slow-combusting gaiety.

To the shepherd and the horseman, the great bell-makers of Aldbourne one hundred and thirty years ago were as famous as Chippendale or Buhl to those in other walks of life. They had music with them, and matched their bells with infinite pride to harmonise in the sheepcote or the elm-lined lane.

5
THE CRAFTSMEN

By Bernard Hollowood

A recent issue of *The New Yorker* contained advertisements for:

Tweeds – 'Imported and hand-woven Scottish tweed – a fine mixture of tweed and imagination.'

Woollen sweaters – 'Hand-fashioned and expressly knitted for Rogers Peet by one of Scotland's most celebrated makers.'

Shirts – 'Imported English broadcloth shirts . . . woven and finished in England with painstaking care.'

Silver – 'Made to our order in England where they know the art so well . . . heavy silver-plate on copper.'

Ale – 'The product of 200 years' British brewing experience.'

Flannels – 'England's finest fabrics – tailored by hand in our own workshops . . .'

Shortbread – 'As Scottish as "Auchtermuchty" . . . and easier to ask for . . . favorite for six generations.'

Bread – 'A byword in England for over 50 years.'

Scents – 'Created in England . . . from the original English formulae . . .

Waistcoats – 'Authentic clan colorings imported from Scotland.'

Glass – 'Hand-blown English cut-crystal of pure craftsmanship.'

Soap – 'The original Windsor . . .'

Pottery – 'Charming rendition of this fine Old English pattern.'

Raincoats – 'The standard by which all other weathercoats are judged, an original, imported from England.'

All these in addition to fulsome puffs for British cars, bicycles, dufflecoats, socks, cigarettes, whisky, gin, jam, shoes, marmalade, biscuits, and butterscotch.

A trained investigator of the Gallupian breed could work wonders with these ads. He would examine the incidence of the adjectives; he would put frequency tabs on such keywords as 'original', 'Old English' and 'Olde Englishe', 'hand-made', and 'craftsmanship'. And I should be vastly impressed by his findings. For the moment, however, while I sit back and applaud the remarkable success of

Right: Mrs. Macdonald of South Uist in the Outer Hebrides spinning the thread of Harris tweed

Henry Cole claimed to be the begetter of the Great Exhibition of 1851. William Morris vomited when he saw it

the British manufacturer's assault on dollar market No. 1, I must make do without the statistical fruits of such deep scrutiny.

It is clear, though, that British goods appeal most strongly in America when attention is drawn to their age, their authenticity and the high degree of craftsmanship that has gone into their making. How much of this is based on sentiment, nostalgia or snob-appeal it is difficult to say, but there comes a time, quite obviously, when the citizens of a neotechnic society tire of their precise, mass-produced physical environment and yearn for the authentic smell of Harris tweed and the village forge, the sounds of the silversmith's hammer and the hand-weaver's loom, and the quality, yes, the *quality*, of hand-blown glassware, thrown pottery, 'home-made' marmalade and shortbread – in other words, for the *wares* of the craftsman instead of the products and merchandise of the engineer, scientist, design consultant and machine-minder.

We need not, of course, accept 'traditional British craftsmanship' as anything more than a clever advertising stunt. It can be argued – and some of the findings of the Anglo-American Council on Productivity would lend support to the argument – that British industry is on the whole relatively inefficient by American standards, that much of our plant and machinery and most of our manufacturing methods are out-of-date, that we have allowed the grass to grow under our feet, lathes and looms. It *can* be argued that the quality of 'craftsmanship' in our goods is entirely bogus and worthless, that what we and the Americans are deceived into praising as the marks of sound hand-work are really the imperfections of inefficient and out-moded machine processes.

There may be a grain of truth in the assumption; but only a grain.

No, says the economist of school B, the quality of craftsmanship is not strained: it is

A chest designed by Phillip Webb and decorated by Morris with paintings in the mediaeval manner, c. 1880

the result of British industry's inevitable devotion to small batch production. Our markets are world-wide and infinitely varied. Unlike the mass-producers of the United States, for whom exports are merely an overflow from a huge home market, our manufacturers must seek to satisfy the tastes of customers in every zone, on almost every parallel of latitude. Our productive resources must, therefore, be kept flexible and adaptable, and our operatives must be capable of switching rapidly from one job to another. Craftsmanship is in effect a reflection of our relatively small-scale production and of the versatility of our workers. It is something very real and valuable.

There is certainly something in that.

Craftsmanship, says the historian, is the fruit of traditional skills. For centuries Britain has been a sanctuary for the oppressed peoples of Europe. Religious and racial persecutions and economic duress have driven thousands of skilled craftsmen to these islands – carpet-weavers, potters, glass-blowers, wood-workers, clock-makers, jewellers, tailors, silk-weavers, goldsmiths and silversmiths, bakers, candlestickmakers . . . and their know-how, their manipulative dexterity and aesthetic sensibility has become part of our own tradition. Not, of course, that the native English were duffers. To build their fine churches they had to master stone; to build the wooden walls of England they had to master oak. British goods exhibit fine craftsmanship for no other reason than that they are made by craftsmen. In the same way America became a refuge for Europeans in the nineteenth and twentieth centuries, but these latter-day emigrants were scientists, technologists and engineers. Britain got the Elers brothers; America, Einstein.

There is a lot in that.

But what is this craftsmanship? Is it the thumb-marks on a thrown vase, the dents of the hammer in beaten silverware, the marks

Above: Inside the Crystal Palace during the Great Exhibition. *Right:* Singular exhibits: sportsman's jack-knife with eighty blades and tools, bedstead in zebra wood, and grand centre portion of a service of plate

of the chisel on wood, the file on steel, the paintbrush on china? Can it be that the hand, as a tool or as a chuck to hold a tool, has some mysterious advantage over the machine? Is there a harmony between the material and the form and the purpose of an article made by hand that is beyond the power of the machine to imitate? 'Many simple tools have this look . . .' Walter Dorwin Teague has written. 'Generation after generation has contributed to their refinement, perfecting their forms until no further improvement is possible and they take their places beside the forms of nature. An ax helve, so gracefully curved in its strange shape, a plowshare, an ox yoke, a hay wain, swords and helmets, bells and pots, a thousand simple objects that have been in use over long periods of time, have arrived at this satisfactory perfection of form. By trial and error – the endless trials and eliminated errors of countless painstaking craftsmen – beauty has been achieved.'

Integrity, infallible co-ordination between hand and eye, experience backed by tradition, and pride in a job well done – these are the conventional attributes of craftsmanship. The words 'operative' and 'employee' evoke mental pictures of clocking-on machines, conveyers, assembly lines, shop stewards, time-and-motion study hawks, jigs, templates, canteens and steel furniture, welfare officers and grey-faced machinists; the word 'craftsman' suggests a leather apron, dusty bull's eye windows giving on to grass and trees, children looking in at the open door, an old meerschaum pipe, steel-rimmed spectacles, grey hair, simple tools worn smooth by centuries of use, spit and polish. Grey hair. *Yes, somehow all our remaining craftsmen are old-timers:* lovable, vaguely comic characters like oldest

Bill Slingsby, of Sussex, manufacturer of hurdles and pit-props, removing the bark from chestnut wood with a hoople shave, and a Penshurst craftsman making cricket balls at Wisden's famous Kent workshops

inhabitants and absent-minded professors.

Crabbed age listening to a cuckoo-clock: disillusioned youth waiting for the factory-hooter.

William Morris would surely say 'I told you so.' He was only seventeen when he vomited after one quick look at the machine-age art exhibited so proudly at the Crystal Palace. It was possibly the most justifiable act of vomiting in history. Unfortunately Morris founded a school of arty-crafty retchers and vomiters and they are still with us. Or, rather, they are not with us: our Morrisite artist-craftsmen live apart from the main stream of society in high-walled clinics of mediaeval art. Their cat's whisker sensitivity and craftsmanship produce fine, elaborate, sophisticated souvenirs which only they, and the ghost of William Morris, can afford or appreciate. The very thought of machinery turns their stomachs.

What is so sad is not that they have taken the wrong turning – for the most part they live happy and contented lives, and keep the peace – but that their exceptional talents should be withheld from public service. They could, so easily, apply them to the improvement of design and quality in the pots, pans, furniture and fittings of everyday life. They could, given the ability to swallow down their hatred of the machine, help to stimulate a revolution in industrial design. They could help the *genuine* craftsmen – by which I mean the blacksmiths, the glass-blowers, the sign-writers and so on – to improve their work. A pity; for they have nothing to lose but their nausea.

Morris's trouble was, of course, his ostrich mentality. He fought the machine by burying his head in Mediaevalism, by rooting himself emotionally in the past. The Luddites, who

Above: Severn putcher baskets used as eel traps, and a Gloucestershire blacksmith erecting his clock made from scrap iron in Eldersfield church. *Below:* Bill Willmser, saddler of Droxford – Allied Invasion H.Q. in June 1944

Sonny Springett, Royal Signwriter and Decorator, paints the blue and white arms first granted to him by Royal Warrant in King George V's reign. Sonny has worked in Windsor Castle ever since he was a boy

regarded the machines with equal vehemence, took positive action: they resorted to violence in a hopeless attempt to stay the monster. But Morris could only back-pedal, retreat and gather disciples on the way.

Yet it is unfair to censure Morris too heavily. None of his contemporaries saw the horrors of 'applied art' more clearly, and none offered any alternative remedy to his pitiful avoiding action. Looking back – from our Dome of Discovery, let's say – it is astounding that the Early Victorians could have been so totally lacking in perception. They were all unhappy about the machine's threat to manual craftsmanship, and many of them realized that the *mariage de convenance* arranged between art and industry had turned out a ghastly flop. But their scientific and mechanical marvels made them forget the standards of integrity set by eighteenth-century architects, builders and craftsmen, and left them unaware of the missing link between machine reproduction and craftsmanship.

And this is true even of Henry Cole, another celebrated craftsman. Cole, who claimed to be the begetter of the Great Exhibition (though Queen Victoria thought otherwise) came nearer than any of his contemporaries to anticipating the work of the industrial designer of the twentieth century. He was a man of prodigious vitality and versatility: at the Post Office he helped to introduce penny postage and himself designed stamps. He painted goodish water colours, etched, wrote and illustrated books of all kinds, potted, engraved, campaigned for Free Trade and a uniform railway gauge, dominated the proceedings of the Royal Society of Arts and set up in business as a producer of 'Art Manufactures'. In 1846 the Royal Society of Arts

 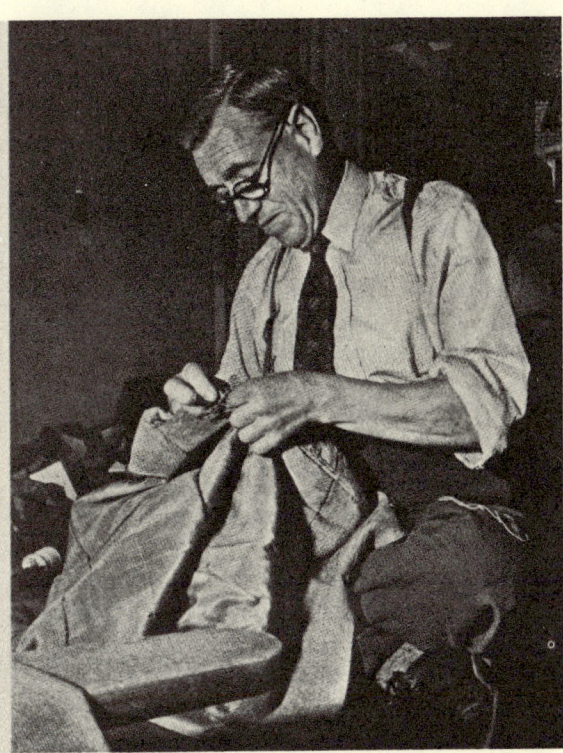

Above: Ede and Ravenscroft, wigmakers for ten generations in Chancery Lane, and a bespoke tailor's workman in London's West End. *Below:* Charles Slate, who carved the entrance doors for the new House of Commons

offered prizes for the best new designs for a number of articles in common domestic use – including a tea-service and beer mugs. And Cole, as Miss Yvonne ffrench has told us (in *The Great Exhibition*: 1891, Harvill Press), 'rushed to compete. He seized hold of Herbert Minton, the china manufacturer, a reluctant participator who dreaded the tyranny of London retailers, and talked him into submitting a design for beer mugs. He himself set to work on the tea-set.' He hurried to Stoke-on-Trent where he supervised the modelling and production of the 'Summerly Tea-service' ('Felix Summerly' was Cole's *nom de guerre*) and in due course exhibited it at the Adelphi rooms. It won the Society's silver medal, earned widespread approval, and sold like hot cakes for many years.

To the customer of 1951 the Summerly Tea-service would seem ordinary and perhaps familiar: it was austere, plain and white, and except for a few odd quirks of classicism – the milk-jug, for example, was remarkable for its three-lipped Etruscan neck – it was not vastly inferior to genuine modern 'utility'. It was fashioned in accordance with principles first enumerated by Cole and his coterie – 'plainness, cheapness, elegance and beauty commensurate with cost'. There was no mention of usefulness or functional efficiency.

The Prince Consort praised it, commended the fine craftsmanship of the potters of Stoke-on-Trent and urged the Society to press on with its task of improving working-class taste. What Morris thought of it I do not know.

Morris's and Cole's myopia becomes even more astonishing when we reflect that less than a hundred years earlier the great Josiah Wedgwood had taught the world virtually all there is to know about industrial craftsmanship in general and about the craft of potting in particular. And if this statement sounds extravagant it can only be modified to this extent – that 'Josiah Wedgwood' symbolises all

Below: By Royal Appointment, Brierly crystal glass has been made by the same firm for four Sovereigns. *Right*: Sword, designed and made by Leslie Durbin: a gift to Lord Tedder from the Corporation of the City of London

those who worked with him, his artists, modellers, throwers and makers, as well as a number of his rivals in manufacture. We can do no better, if we wish to study British craftsmanship at close quarters, then to turn back to the chapter in economic and commercial history entitled 'Josiah Wedgwood'.

First, though, we must know something of his medium. Clay, apparently so docile and malleable, is probably the least tractable of all materials. It is almost animate in its fractiousness. It refuses to submit to the strait-jacket of scientific production controls and nurses its idiosyncrasies like an old bachelor. And when the potter seeks to tame it for all time in the great heat of the oven it shrinks visibly and tries to writhe out of shape.

It is this delinquent stubbornness of clay that makes the potter's job so stimulating and, by turns, so enjoyable and so exasperating; and it is because clay can only be handled satisfactorily by 'green fingers' that potting remains a craft even in these days of large-scale factory production. The complete potter must be much more than a modeller: he must master the physics, chemistry and pyrometry of clays, glazes and ceramic colours; he must be familiar with clay's reactions to stress and strain and heat. He must know it as the painter knows his palette and as the bridge-builder knows his steel.

Josiah Wedgwood was the complete potter.

He was born in Burslem, Staffordshire, in 1730, of a long line of potters and part-time potters. In those days pottery was made throughout Britain, wherever suitable clays could be dug and enough fuel found, and the wares of Burslem were mostly crude salt-glazed butter-pots, dishes and jugs made from the local red marls. Josiah left school at the age of nine and at fourteen was apprenticed by his brother Thomas to 'the Art, Mistery, Occupation or Imployment of Thrower and Handleing.'

It was this simple peasant handicraft that Wedgwood and his contemporaries translated into a world-famous craft-industry. In his 'Experiment Book', which was begun in the

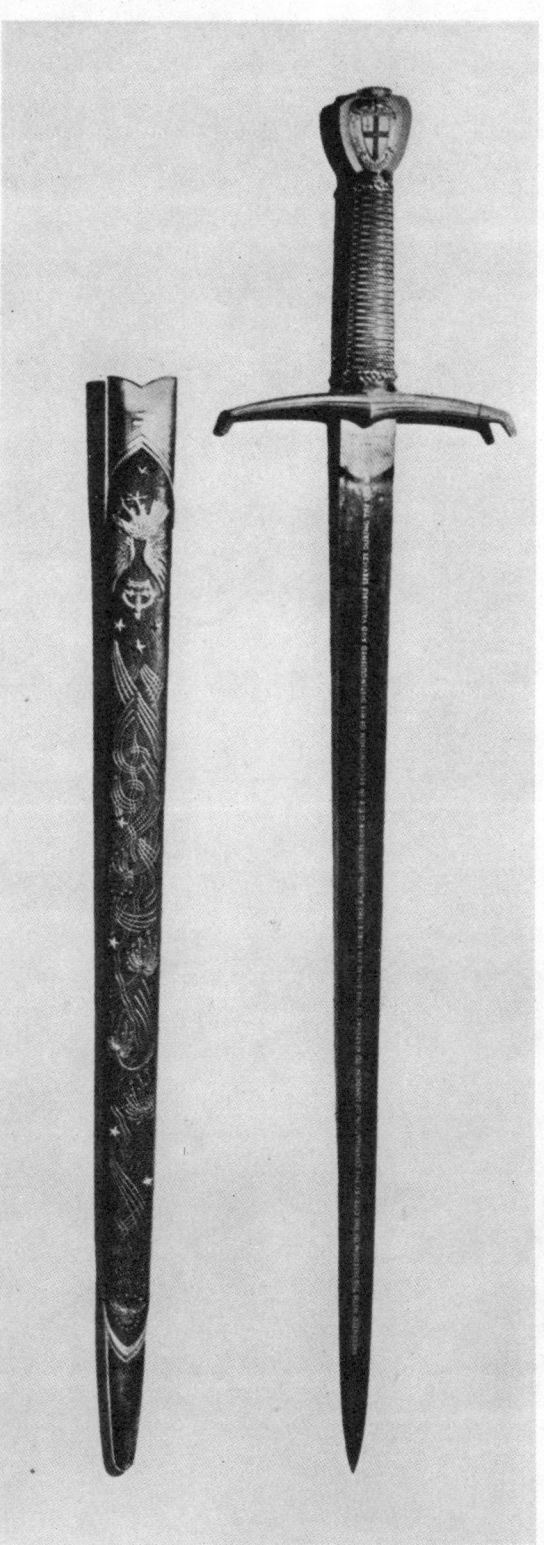

55

'fifties during his partnership with Whieldon, Wedgwood outlined the scope of his early work:

'This suite of Experiments was begun at Fenton Hall, in the parish of Stoke-on-Trent, about the beginning of the year 1759, in my partnership with Mr. Whieldon, for the improvement of our manufacture of earthenware, which at the time stood in great need of it, the demand for our goods decreasing daily, and the trade universally complained of as being bad and in a declining condition.

'White stone ware was the principal article of our manufacture. But this had been made a long time, and the prices were now reduced so low, that the potters could not afford to bestow much expense upon it or to make it so good in any respect as the ware would otherwise admit of. And with regard to elegance of form, that was an object very little attended to.

'The next article in consequence to Stone Ware was an imitation of Tortoiseshell. But as no improvement had been made in this branch for several years, the country had grown weary of it; and though the price had been lowered from time to time in order to increase the sale, the expedient did not answer, and something was wanted, to give a little spirit to the business.

'I have already made an imitation Agate, which was esteemed beautiful and a considerable improvement, but people were surfeited with wares of these variegated colours.

'These considerations induced me to try for some more solid improvements, as well in the Body, as the Glazes, the Colours and the Forms of the articles of our manufacture.

'I saw the field was spacious, and the soil so good as to promise an ample recompense to any one who should labour diligently in its cultivation.'

A very revealing document. Clearly, there was nothing of the dilettante, the arty-crafty or the ivory-towered Morris in Wedgwood's make-up. Craftsmanship meant the exercise of hand, eye, brain, taste and business acumen. It meant hard work, experiment, adventure and, with luck, profits. It meant the creation of wares of high quality and wide acceptability – not the stuffy, self-conscious systematised fidgeting of the Morris brigade. The complete potter was marvellously equipped. He had the cool penetrative mind of the rationalist, the fervour of the true artist, the shrewdness of the Midlands business man and these qualities were allied to a voracious appetite for knowledge (he was a member of that early Brains Trust, the Lunar Society, which met monthly, usually in Birmingham, by the light of the full moon, and which included such leading figures as Boulton and Watt; Joseph Priestley; Whitehurst, the clockmaker and geologist; Erasmus Darwin; Withering, the botanist; Keir, the glassmaker; Richard Lowell Edgworth, and Thomas Day) and a genuine enthusiasm for humanitarian reforms. A catalogue of his achievements as a craftsman is impressive. 'He built bigger and better kilns; he improved the wheel and introduced the turning lathe which enabled the potter to give finish and precision to his wares; he investigated and vastly improved the chemical constituents of clays and glazes; he discovered new types of wares, such as "black basaltes" and "jasper"; he invented a pyrometer for measuring the heat of the furnace . . .' (Herbert Read, *Art and Industry*, Faber and Faber) and, in addition, and as we are only now beginning to discover, he was himself an excellent designer and modeller.

Until quite recently Wedgwood's great reputation has rested almost entirely with his neo-classic re-creations, the facsimile reproductions of the vases and sculptures of Greek and Roman antiquity. In his day and for a century after his death the Wedgwood Jasper wares epitomized the art of the nation, just as ceramic urns had once represented the artistic genius of ancient Greece.

His 'Portland Vase' was hailed as miraculous and pluperfect. 'I have compared the copy of the Portland Vase with the original,' wrote Sir Joshua Reynolds, in a statement that reads suspiciously like a modern unsolicited testimonial to the manufacturers of some patent cure for eczema or baldness, 'and I can

Left: Josiah Wedgwood, 1951. Behind him, the first Josiah Wedgwood, 1730–95, painted by Reynolds

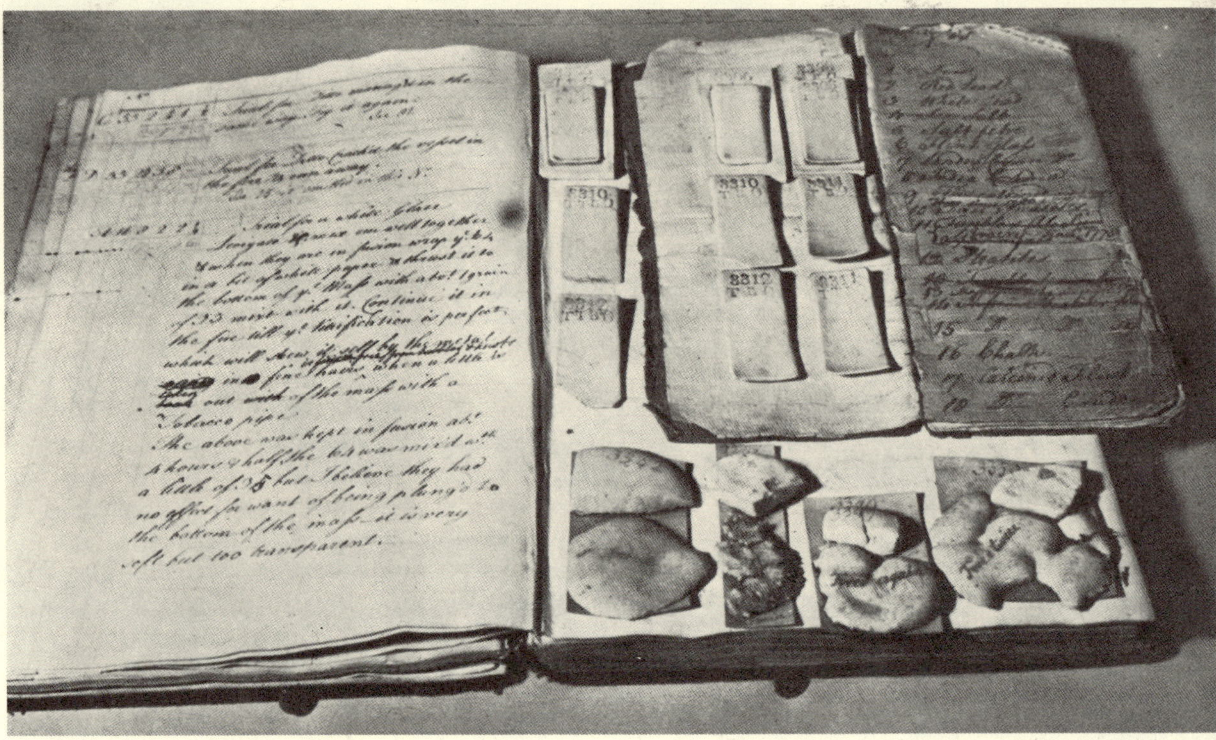

Above: 'The complete potter's' Experiment Book with the Wedgwood formulae in code. *Below:* 'The Art, Mistery, Occupation or Imployment of Thrower and Handleing': the modelling room at Etruria, about 1790

declare it to be a correct and faithful imitation.' As an example of copybook workmanship it was indeed superb, like so many of his classical simulacra. But it was not, in the true sense of the word, good potting.

In many of the basaltes and jaspers the clay was forced into unsuitable moulds, made to adopt forms created in other media – glass, marble or metal. And their decoration, though brilliantly executed, lacked the spontaneity and charm that had characterised the ceramic brushwork of the Chinese and Egyptian masters of potting. The jaspers and basaltes were precise, mathematically perfect creations which harmonised admirably with the contemporary architecture of Adam and the furniture of Chippendale and Hepplewhite; but their beauty was cold, academic and secondhand.

These are, of course, personal views. I was born within a china stone's throw of the site of the Churchyard Works where Wedgwood began his career; I grew up among the marl-banks and shraff-tips of the Potteries; I lectured for some years at the Wedgwood Institute and studied at the Wedgwood Museum; and like all 'potters' I became intensely proud of the pottery industry and its greatest figure. Yet, if I had to assess Wedgwood's genius solely on the strength of his ornamental wares I should not put it very much higher than that of Bernard Palissy or Bernard Moore.

For me, Wedgwood's true greatness rests with his so-called 'Useful Wares', the table services in 'Cream Colour' or 'Queen's Ware'. These wares, many of them designed and modelled by the master himself, exhibited all the true properties of clay: they were the works of an original craftsman in complete control of his material, an artist content to allow beauty to grow from the perfect solution to a practical problem and his own unconscious aesthetic sensibility. They were 'extremely simple, neat, convenient and durable' and they became the prototypes of the finest practical wares made by potters throughout the world. Many of Josiah's shapes and patterns

Above: The tradition of useful wares. Mug, 1695, found at Burslem: Staffordshire tankard, *c.* 1725: Wedgwood mug designed in 1940 by Eric Ravilious

59

are still in production at Barlaston; and they are still best sellers. Under the direction of Josiah's great-great-great-grandson (another Josiah Wedgwood) the great tradition has been strengthened and enriched. The new shapes and patterns emerging from the Barlaston studios match the 'Useful Wares' for workmanship, usefulness and felicitous line and pattern. There can be no higher praise.

Pottery, as we have seen, is one of the few important industries in Britain that still calls for craftsmanship of the traditional type. In other industries the economic division of labour has simplified and mechanized the processes of production so completely that very few operatives are now capable of much more than a single, speedy, specialized act of construction or assembly. The machine has triumphed, as Morris feared it would, and most of the problems it poses are as far from solution as they were a hundred years ago. In many industries the joy of creative craftsmanship has gone for ever (though, to be fair, we must admit that the old forms of craftsmanship were not always creative, and that all repetitive jobs eventually become joyless): it has been replaced by shorter working hours, 'social security', and cheap canned entertainment. In his later years Morris was compelled, reluctantly and against his better judgement, to admit that machines could be useful. 'Those almost miraculous machines,' he wrote, 'which if orderly forethought had dealt with them might even now be speedily extinguishing all irksome and unintelligent labour, leaving us free to raise the standard of skill of hand and energy of mind in our workmen, to produce afresh that loveliness and order which only the hand of man guided by his own soul can produce; what have they

In the shadow of the giant factories, the old-time craftsman feels insignificant, a survival of another age

done for us?' To Morris machines were but muck-shifters and sledge-hammers: their only virtue was that they might rescue men from drudgery and allow them more time in which to practise the arts of creative handicrafts.

So far, however, there have been few signs that men are eager to spend their increased leisure in this way. Most of them seem content to leave creative work to industrial designers, and reproduction to the machine, while they themselves seek excitement or relaxation via football and football pools, greyhounds, the cinema, radio and television. But wait! Didn't some American efficiency expert tell us the other day that British workmen are taking too much out of themselves at home? And didn't he suggest that all those odd jobs, like wallpapering, piano-shifting, cabinet-fixing, picture framing and hanging, plumbing, pointing and painting, ought to be done by accredited practitioners? Oh, yes, and gardening.

Well, there may be something in it. The British workman may, for all I know, still exercise his flair for craftsmanship by good husbandry, and his efforts in the home may, possibly, reduce his efficiency in the factory. I can only counter these allegations by quoting the wife of the writer of this article: 'You never lift a finger . . !' she usually begins.

As I was saying – before I was so rudely interrupted by these irrelevancies – the machine is steadily killing off what is left of our traditional manual of craftsmanship. In the neotechnic factories most of the workers are robots: 'fifteen minutes for lunch, three minutes to go to the toilet, the Taylorized speedup everywhere, reach under, adjust washer, screw down bolt, shove in cotterpin, reach-under adjustwasher, screwdownbolt, reach-underadjustscrewdown, reachunderadjust . . .'

Proud of a three-hundred-year old tradition, Mrs. Honeysett's family has made watches since Charles II's days

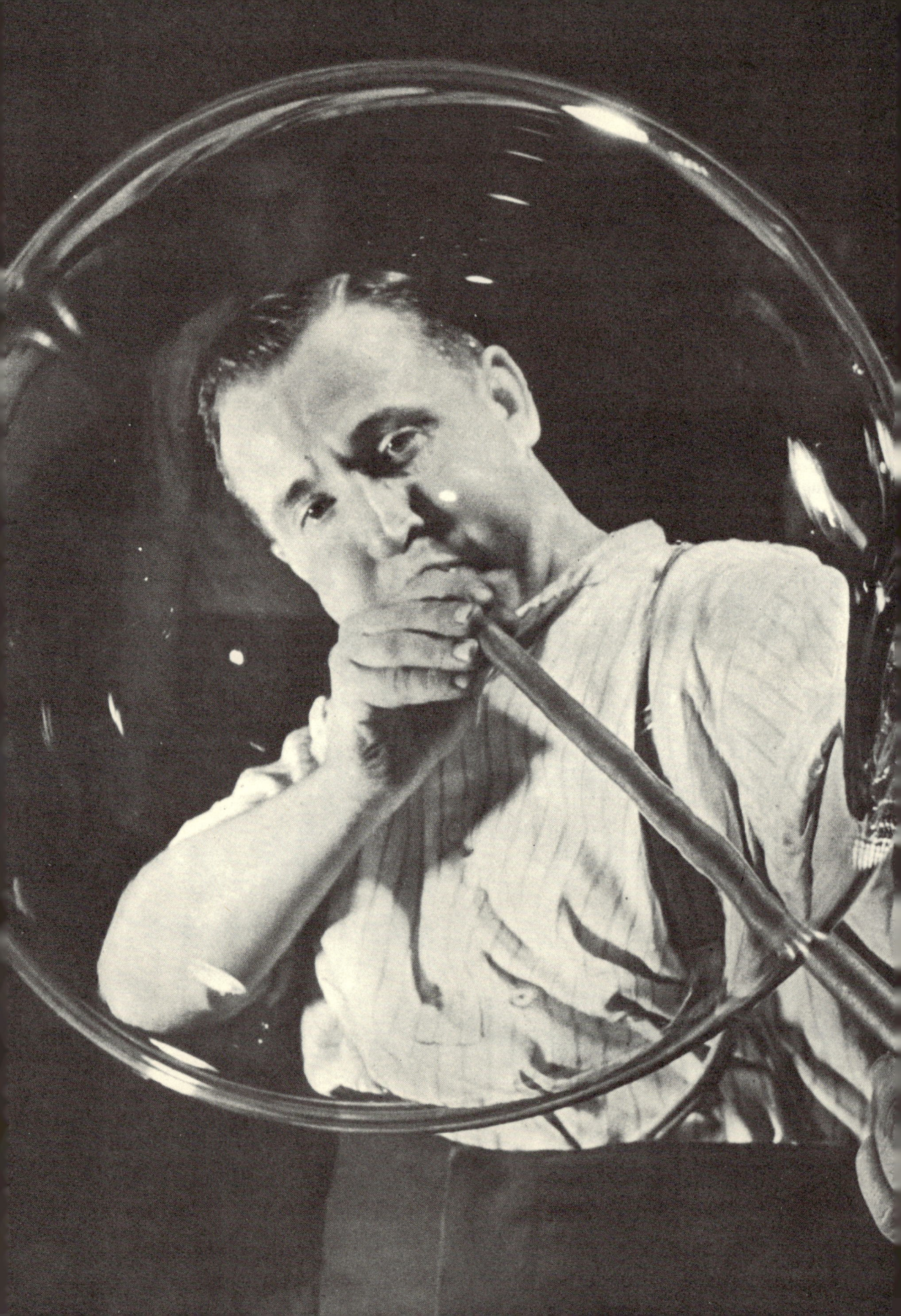

Make slight adjustments to John Dos Passos's picture of American factory labour, make it an hour and a quarter for lunch and half an hour each way for a smoke – and you have the British counterpart.

But machine reproduction does not mean an end to craftsmanship; only a change in its distribution. In the modern factory all the creative thought and handwork is concentrated in the key-men, in the handful of people who make decisions, design machinery, products, production schedules.... The division of labour has finally resolved itself into an unfair distribution of opportunities for the exercise of creative talents – and there is nothing, apparently, that we can do about it.

For twelve months I have been examining traditional British craftsmanship at close quarters. I have visited small manufactories of hand-woven silks, damasks, brocades, tweeds and carpets, of hand-forged silverware, hand-wrought iron, hand-blown and hand-cut crystal glassware, hand-thrown pottery and hand-made hats, furniture, paper, tobacco pipes, confectionery, boots and shoes and many more goods. In all of these establishments, without exception, I have found the working conditions good, the atmosphere healthy and the craftsmen infinitely proud of their work. Yet in nearly every case the number of workers is steadily shrinking. It is impossible, I am told, to find enough new recruits to keep these old crafts full manned, and difficult enough to prevent trained craftsmen (under forty years of age) from downing their tools and seeking fresh employment in the big factories.

Why?

The reasons are psychological, I think, rather than economic. The new sense of freedom engendered by conditions of full employment, the slightly higher wages paid in the factories, the pull of the big trade unions – all these things may have some effect; much more important, however, is the fact that the worker feels he is improving his status by moving from the little workshop to the assembly lines. He imagines – quite wrongly of course – that employment in the big factories is somehow more dignified than employment in the potting-shop and the glasshouse. In the factory he controls, or appears to control, masses of intricate and costly machinery, and feels commensurately important and powerful; in the village smithy he works with equipment that was used by his father and grandfather and under conditions that have not altered appreciably for hundreds of years, and thinks himself a stick-in-the-mud.

In the shadow of the giant factory the craftsman feels insignificant, a pottering survival from another age.

Boys no longer want to be glass-blowers and hand-loom weavers when they grow up. They want to be mechanics, engineers, machinists; they want to be 'on production'. 'Smiths' and 'wrights' are out of fashion.

And it is very sad.

Left : The glass-blower of Stourbridge, Worcestershire, where they have been making glass since 1556

6
HEART OF FIRE

By Roy Lewis

If you say to a film director: 'I am making a film called "This Britain". Let's start with heavy industry. Make me a picture sequence which shall suggest the power, the drive, the drama of industrial life,' he will know exactly what to do. The odds are that he has done it before. He will collect close-up shots of machine after machine, of conveyor-line after conveyor-line, of factories going up, miners going down, furnaces being tapped and blazing like fireworks, oil or plastics or chocolate pouring glutinously from nozzles, women working in a spider-web of spinning machinery, men wrestling with white-hot wire like Laocoon & Sons with the snakes, the Brabazon in the air and (inevitably) the *Queen Elizabeth* at sea. He will then cunningly interlace them, using camera angle, panning shots, and fast cutting to give an overwhelming effect of stuff in general being chewed, chopped, spat, split, smashed, ripped, cut, boiled, and sewed and riveted together again, *andante, allegro, presto, prestissimo*, (Ravel's *Bolero* or de Falla's *Fire Dance* provide the inevitable choice of accompaniment) until, upon the last chords, the *Queen Elizabeth* steams majestically New Yorkwards, supreme embodiment of that vast forge and smithy, modern industrial Britain. And all in about seven minutes of showing-time.

Indeed, when I close my eyes and set the stimulus word 'industry', some such succession of images asserts itself. In my case, however, they are true after-images, because I have spent so much of my life footsore from plodding round factories, deafened by rolling-mills, scorched by the breath of furnaces, and sooted-up by coal dust or other industrial emanations. You know, perhaps, how after an evening spent playing chess, when you compose yourself for sleep, the chequer-board and nearly discernible positions of the pieces are thrown on the faintly-luminous mind's eye. You are tantalized to grasp the problem. It is so with a man who visits factories at the rate of two or more a week. If I die by drowning, it is British industry, performing every possible operation upon steel, nonferrous metals, tex-

Right: A strip mill at Ebbw Vale. In 1950 Britain produced over 1,500,000 tons of sheet steel

Working night and day, Llandarcy oil refinery in South Wales is one of many British post-war refineries

tile fibres, and the whole gamut of synthetic substances, which will pass before my mind. Perhaps I shall then find a split second in which to regret I didn't become a Church historian.

But it is a false picture. That's machinery, not the heart and soul of either light or heavy industry; the accidents, not the substance. Well, what is the substance? Can I define it, convey it in words, pick some one incident or story or conversation, which will put it over as a quality of living, just as country life has its quality, savoursome and various by county and clime? And can I do that, avoiding alike the grey groping polysyllables of the economist and the schweppervescent blah of the advertising copywriter ('Industry brings you the *goods*, the sturdy, hardwearing stuff with the built-in craftsmanship which goes with the famous words "Made in Britain"...')?

I don't know. But let me go on drowning. Let me sink a little deeper into my past. The factories are getting more out-of-date, now, than even an American industrial consultant would expect. I am back in my childhood, twenty-five, nearly thirty years ago, a childhood spent mainly in Birmingham and in the genial shade of a father who was a Birmingham business man, a man to whom doing a thing and getting enthusiastic about it were part of the same process of life – a carry-over in some degree from the years he had spent schoolmastering before he joined a chemical firm. A schoolmaster-business man. An admirable beginning. In Britain you will meet schoolmaster-business men, soldier-business men, novelist-business men, University don-business men, craftsman-business men, artist-business men, explorer-business men, and many other exotic cross-fertilizations, besides the general run of just business men and big business men. Yes, and you can meet them in Birmingham.

Walter Rathenau said somewhere: 'I have never yet met with a business man whose chief aim was to acquire wealth. I will even go so far as to assert that he who is out to make

It takes three of these giant ladles to fill a 200-ton steel ingot mould in Sheffield, the home of 'special' jobs

money cannot possibly be a great business man.' At first glance, no less suitable city for proving the truth of Rathenau's generalisation could be selected than Birmingham. Birmingham loves money, simply adores it. I well remember my father's scorn when the Birmingham Municipal Savings Bank first chose for its motto, 'He that has, is.' But they changed it. Birmingham sacked the great Dr. Joseph Priestley's house; Birmingham never had enough civic pride, not to say religion, to build a cathedral; Birmingham is all shiny cars, all nicely-calculated less or more, all imitation jewelry. Or so you may think: all business. But it isn't, and my father, who took the attack on Priestley, discoverer of oxygen, in 1791 practically as a personal matter, proved it to me. In one of the innumerable places where they make 'made-in-Brummagem' jewelry, he found a middle-aged man calmly decorating gold ornaments with tiny gold granules in the Etruscan manner. The secret had been lost three thousand years. The craftsman had rediscovered it – for a hobby; and he had no idea that the *Illustrated London News* would be glad to devote two pages of photographs to his achievement.

A few miles further on, there was the man whom *Punch* later described as 'the man who put the ming in Birmingham.' It *was* Ming. He rediscovered the Chinese method of glazing – and produced pieces which deceived experts. But he sold the lovely things he made simply as 'Ruskin ware' – and most of it went as made-in-Britain stuff to America. He earned dollars for Britain. It may be said that such survivals of a craftsman's joy in his work cannot redeem Birmingham; I say they do, for I could quote a score of cases. And the native craftsmanship went into so many other things, which you might call simply industrial. Back to me comes my father's grin on the day after a certain Mr. Royce had visited the works, to buy sheet for the radiators of Rolls Royce cars. He merely said, however good their finish, they must do still better for Rolls

Britain makes over a third of the world's merchant ships. A Clydeside welder, and (*right*) a Belfast shipyard

Royce. They did. They sent Mr. Royce jobs of work of which he never complained (naturally, he never praised them; that would never do!). Today that factory does the metallurgical work which makes the jet engine possible; the selfsame care and craftsmanship, mated with science, has overcome the problems of producing metal parts able to stand terrific temperatures. And it was the perfectionism of the Rolls Royce tradition, manifested in even the finish of the 'RR' radiator, which made the Derwent and the Nene engines the amazingly efficient power-units that they are.

Memories come back from the days when my father was in chemicals, before he went into metals. I remember talk of the Swedish match octopus, and Birmingham's determination not to be eaten by it (nor was it); and mingled with talk of Krueger, there was talk of a new medium for painters (which was not taken up) and a flare to be dropped by airmen when they sought for the flight deck of a carrier in the dark (which, pioneered in the twenties, saved the lives of hundreds of young airmen in World War II). Sometimes my father was up in the air, dropping flares in the Solent; sometimes he was outside the clerestory of Ely Cathedral saving the stone from damage; sometimes he was on the Continent wrestling with chemical cartels but finding time to study the preservation of frescoes in Italian churches; sometimes he was dealing darkly with poison gases. That's Birmingham business as I grew up to know it – imitative and inventive, greedy and openhanded by turns, a Philistine mask, craftsmanship living in the hand, and integrity ruling the heart. A waste of slums which produced truth and beauty in everyday things, quality and character in men.

Incredible as it may seem to those who stand on the down platform of New Street Station for the first time, or who catch their first sight of the black Municipal Parthenon in which the city fathers deliberate, the joy of making things supplies the drive in Birmingham. In thousands of small workshops they make things the world could not be without – today, as in the days of John Leyland, Henry VIII's antiquary, 'There be many smiths in the towne that use to make knives and all manour of cutting tooles, and many lorimers

that make bittes and a great many naylours.' But Birmingham also has the largest conveyor-line making cars outside Detroit. Birmingham is endlessly surprising, full of contrasts. The last time I was there I saw a forge – a forge, of all filthy things! – in a factory made of glass, absolutely clean glass. When Birmingham has finished doing things like that to itself the black country will cease to be black for the first time since Henry VIII's day. And that, to bring back the green grass, and the blue sky, and the clear crystal stream, will be as noble as to build a cathedral. It may be a dream, but I don't put it past Birmingham.

It's a messy business, creation; but as man is made in his Creator's image and therefore fore-ordained to create, we must expect mess, we must expect Birminghams, Sheffields, Glasgows, and (perhaps most terrible of all) Government Trading Estates. Man, I suppose, makes a bigger mess in his creative efforts than God does, but man is in a frightful hurry and lacks experience. The result is industrial Britain. It's a mess we ought to clear up as best we can, but do not let us condemn industrialism – making things – on the mean streets of Birmingham and Sheffield alone. Agriculture is just as bad in the early stages of learning how to do things – it was bad grassland management which has turned so much of the Middle East into desert. Now nothing grows in the heart of that desert; but things do grow in every dreary industrial town in Britain. They grow inside the factories, and if you want to know the real life of these places, you must find out what the people in them are doing, planning, thinking, dreaming of, quarrelling about, and falling in love with, in these factories. The 'cheap-and-nasty' ones may be making fibre attaché cases (one of which may someday carry a masterpiece to a publisher); the worthier ones may be making mechanisms as exquisite as the human heart.

From all of them come tributaries, small or large, to the river of British industrial invention. Behind every invention there is a man, a life; perhaps a tragedy. I go into few factories without hearing a story which would make a novel, if one could tell it; but how few can find even the palest reflection in print! Industry is secretive; British industry, in particular, hates admitting that before you win a victory you must fight a campaign and that it is in the fighting that the drama lies. A bald announcement that the biggest ship in the world has been built, or the smallest tube in the world has been drawn; but little or nothing about the toil and the tears which preceded these achievements – that would be undignified, or upset the oldest director on the board, or something. And so the realities of private enterprise, of managerial effort, of research and invention are little understood by a public half-gulled into believing big business is powerful, whereas its terror of the Government is abject; that anybody can manage a business if trained at a school of administration, whereas managers are born; that inventions can be made by committees working with a Government grant, whereas no committee ever invented anything, except perhaps a subcommittee.

Don't let us make any mistake about it: mere size is not the measuring-rod wherewith to measure industrial achievement. The only yardstick, or should I say two-yard-stick, is the men who conceive great projects, or control the Brobdingnagian equipment which these projects make necessary. As a matter of fact, the aim of industry is usually smallness and neatness, not size. The four-mile long steel strip mill at Margam in South Wales is the smallest possible to give the product required. The *Queen Elizabeth* and *Queen Mary* are the smallest liners possible to give a weekly transatlantic service with two, instead of (as before) three ships, and so save the Cunard Company's (and the passengers') money. The Brabazon is the smallest aircraft possible to do the *non-stop* transatlantic flight East-West as well as West-East, with an economic payload, in all conditions except the very worst (meaning only 2 per cent of scheduled flights). The problem in business is to solve the problem, not to build the biggest This or That. The problems of making a really good small

Left: The Loch Lomond hydro-electric station brings new power to the Scottish Highlands

'Perfectionism in the Rolls Royce tradition …' in a world - famous car radiator and in the turbine aircraft engine

watch movement are far bigger, for Britain, than those of building the *Queen Elizabeth*!

You cannot spend long in industry without realising that what counts is men, men who can create; keeping up the supply of these is the big problem. Creativity, the divine attribute, is a wayward thing. The wind bloweth where it listeth, and the nation must trim its sails accordingly. How precarious seem the chances that favour each invention when you really dig into the story! Fifteen years ago a young man, self-taught at evening classes, but a brilliant mechanic by instinct, who had been brought up in the hosiery trade at Leicester, was appointed by a large firm to solve a problem: a knitting machine to make stitches three times faster than any built hitherto. The big firm had built the machine, only it didn't work. In fact, it couldn't work unless a thousand miracles a minute could be wrought. After a long struggle, the young man was told that if he couldn't somehow perform these miracles, his job and his colleagues' jobs were forfeit. Immense sums had already been lost. One night, in desperation, he knelt and prayed. What he was praying for was a needle, an absolutely new sort of mechanical needle. The next day, in a second-hand book shop, he was offered for twopence a book on knitting machinery, printed nearly a hundred years before. Idly turning its pages, *he found his needle there* — a high-speed needle which a mechanic like himself had suggested and sketched in principle, but which the metallurgy and machine tools of 1845 could not produce. From that rough sketch arose the fastest knitting machine in the world, knitting at an incredible 1,000 courses a minute. It took another five years to create it, for it demanded a score of subsidiary inventions and mathematics for which University professors had to be fee'd; but it had arrived — *just in time for nylon*.

Samuel Smiles would have loved that story; but you can find one like it in every factory, where there is a man with an enquiring and original mind. I knew a University don who decided to build his own wooden aircraft in the twenties, and was amazed to discover that he was expected to glue it together with fish-glue —

The same perfectionism gave to Britain her acknowledged leadership of the world in jet and turbo-prop aircraft

the same glue that has been in use for several thousand years. The Romans used it, and so did Stradivarius. But the don, who had been doing academic molecular research, refused to put up with it. From his refusal have arisen the most extraordinary new glues — one of which is now used to glue the *metal* frames of the Comet together. Incidentally, he had to create an industrial organisation to carry through his ideas.

Since the war British industry has faced a grand assize, and has been indicted for failing to use the latest American machines and methods. At the same time, we hear that the discoveries of British science are nearly all exploited commercially in America rather than in Britain. There's truth in it, but there's also truth in the retort that taxation keeps British businesses too short of working capital to exploit half the more promising of the ideas which go into their suggestion-boxes. I know, however, of a score of American ideas which had to come to Britain to find backers. Britain has the world's finest long-range radio navigation aid, for ships and aircraft, because a British business man saw a future in an idea thought up by a young American engineer, and backed it to the tune of a million pounds in the war even when the U.S. Army and our War Office had turned it down. It was business that had been making cheap gramophone records which carried that invention to success, by showing British sea-captains that it would work. When the seamen demanded it, the civil servants gave in. Just because a British business man has been selling canned boogie-woogie by the million, it does not mean that he can't envisage what a fogbound collier off the Dogger wants in the way of electronic navigational instruments, any more than you can put it past the Birmingham jewelry-maker to rediscover Etruscan filigree, or a devout Leicestershire mechanic not to take a hint from a hundred-year-old textile manual. They may be making cheap attaché cases in the front workshop and designing arctic packaging and protective clothing at the back.

A don is shocked because he is expected to depend on the molecular attraction of fish-glue at 3,000 feet — another airman loses his leg in a Blériot and is amazed to discover that he is expected to wear a wooden leg. So he sits down to create an aluminium artificial leg with which a one-legged man can go ski-ing. In so doing, he is disgusted to find that he is expected to do up every screw with a screwdriver, so he invents pneumatically-driven screwdrivers almost as light as hand ones. Today you often can't tell if a girl is wearing an artificial leg or not; and without the pneumatic tools you could not have the Comet.

This is British industry as I know it, in my humble capacity as an industrial journalist. Over a hundred years ago the explorer, A. W. Kinglake, was speaking of early Victorian England to a Turkish Pasha. 'I know,' the Pasha cried, 'Whizz! whizz! all by wheels! Whirr! whirr! all by steam!' But that was no more the real story then, than is the film phantasmagoria of machines today. It's honesty, originality, courage in men; and a spark of something else thrown off from the divine grindstone. You'll see it in every tenth face, perhaps, in Birmingham.

7

THE MIDDLE WAY

By The Viscount Hailsham

The paradox of British life is that it is at the same time strongly radical and deeply conservative. We form part of a society truly continuous with that which the Conqueror founded after Hastings, yet this society, traditional in form, has shewn itself capable of almost uninterrupted and cumulative change. An Earl at the reign of Edward III could find his way about at the Coronation of King George VI. A member of the Elizabethan House of Commons would know how to address the Chair, avoid reference to his fellows' names, cause a Bill to be read three times, catch the Speaker's eye, listen to the Gracious Speech. Our judges wear the wigs of the eighteenth century, the robes of mediaeval clerics. The owner of land still holds it in free and common socage of the King. The Archbishop of Canterbury still holds the see of Augustine. The King wears the crown of the Confessor, is anointed with oil from the ampulla, claims direct descent from Egbert. There are no *ci-devants*. There is no *ancien régime*. There are no White British.

This is a position of immense strength.

Even where authority has been successfully challenged as at the Reformation, or the accession of William of Orange, the forms and structure of the ancient order were preserved carefully, and by deliberate policy. The one exception, the Cromwellian Commonwealth, proved, for all its brilliance, an unhappy and ephemeral interlude, followed by violent reaction from its rationalism and drabness.

Yet, as the term is generally understood abroad, the British are not merely conservative. The Restoration of Charles II did not, in the end, mean the defeat of Parliament. We fought the French Revolution, and the bourgeois dictatorship which followed it, but what was the Reform Bill but an attempt, typically English in form, to achieve the ideas of 1789? We have a Government claiming to be Socialist, yet we are among the more determined opponents of Communist Russia, and allies of Capitalist America.

Not, of course, that there is anything inconsistent between a conservatism of form and a radicalism of substance. The trouble is that British custom does not conform to this

Left: The Great Hall of the Middle Temple, a legal foundation since the 14th century

distinction. Our conservatism is not simply one of form, our radicalism not confined to matters of substance. The Monarchy may have softened down to a mere hereditary presidency. Yet it remains a trusteeship which might well prevent a march on London comparable to the March on Rome. No one knows quite what power could safely be exercised by the House of Lords. No one quite knows exactly what power a political majority in the House of Commons would venture to employ. No one quite knows when judges are interpreting custom or enacting new substantive law (although, characteristically, they always scrupulously adhere to the convention which makes them pretend to do the former). Nobody, least of all the lawyers, quite knows in advance what the law of England is. Over our whole jurisprudence the shadowy, impalpable, unpredictable, but none the less real and objective, figure of the Reasonable (but, note, not the Common) Man presides like a tutelary deity. But what is reasonable? What twelve *veri et legales homines* or the Honourable Mr. Justice Spiliken, who may be suffering from gout or have won a football pool or a pigeon race, decide in the circumstances to be reasonable in one particular case.

Our Conservative politicians have always been concerned to show that they are abreast with the times and defend traditional custom by appeal to a popular vote on the hustings. Our radicals defend revolutionary thesis by a studious reference to precedent, and find, in truth, disturbingly respectable radical precedents to quote. It is not enough, although it would be true, to say that the same form of Parliamentary Government has supported in turn a mediaeval principality, a Tudor despotism, a Venetian oligarchy, a Liberal bourgeoisie, a Socialist democracy. It would be more true to claim that the same living, continuous, community had known how to preserve its existence through the changing moods of the centuries, profoundly modified and affected by each of these, yet permitting none to snap the unbroken thread of its organic identity.

The principles of liberty and authority have notoriously struggled for mastery since the beginning of political history.

For a long time it was thought that liberty depended upon the existence of the system of constitutional checks and balances of the seventeenth-century settlement, the executive authority of the Crown being nicely set against the legislature, that of the Upper House counterbalancing that of the Lower, and the judiciary, appointed by the Crown, but legally irremovable except by the assent of Parliament, acting as a counterpoise to both. It was this theory, plausibly held, and carefully rationalised, which gave rise to the American constitution, not so much a genuine republicanism as a fossilized constitutional monarchy, with an elective monarch, and an Upper House designed to preserve the federal principle. But if this indeed was the basis of our liberties it has long since disappeared. Cabinet Government placed the authority of the Crown at the disposal of Parliament. The modern Party system ensured that the powers of Parliament should be exercisable by a bare majority, and Party discipline ensured that, within limits, the power of the majority should be exercised in accordance with the decision of the Cabinet.

If the United States of America can be described as an elective monarchy, the modern working constitution of Britain might be described an an absolute republic under a hereditary president, electing a dictatorship for limited periods with unlimited legal powers of which it never dares to make full use.

Yet, with all this, a number of checks and balances effectively remain. One of the most important of these, undoubtedly, is the continuance of practically independent organs of local Government, and the maintenance by these of the police as a function partly of local authority, and partly of a lay magistracy, but never, outside the metropolis, of the central Government. No Communist Minister of the Interior in a Coalition Government can take office in England, and, by the abuse of the power of the police, pave the way for dictatorship. Moreover, education remains in the hands of the localities, and not of the Ministry. No Fascist Ministry of Education can corrupt the youth by administrative fiat. The County Councils could effectively call his bluff. On the other hand, the Central Government has been reassuringly stern with local dictatorships even of its own persuasion.

The two-Party system is at once the mainspring of political authority and one of the main safeguards of liberty. A French critic recently complained to me about a debate in the present House of Commons in which he said that the presence of several parties in the French Chamber enabled the arguments in debate to carry greater weight. However powerful the speeches, he maintained, the only doubt which existed at the end of a debate in the present House was whether a train from the North had been delayed by fog, or whether the recent invalids could be brought down to vote on a stretcher.

'You have substituted Government by ambulance for Parliamentary Government,' he exclaimed.

None the less there are valuable compensations in fairly strict Party discipline and a two-Party system. A plethora of parties inevitably means that at general elections no one Party need fear the possibility of having to accept the responsibilities of Government. Each may promise what it pleases. No one will ever be in a position to allege that a Government committed to its programme has failed to carry it out, when the election is over, and the real business of politics begins. The new Deputies, elected usually not as the sole representative of a recognizable geographical community but as individuals on a party list for a Constituency returning upwards of 60 members, must bargain amongst themselves as to the composition and as to the policy of a new Cabinet; and when in due course the new Cabinet takes over the seals of office its members own an embarrassing and dual loyalty to their Cabinet colleagues whose secrets they

Lord Jowitt, in his Lord Chancellor's robes, leaving the Judge's service held every year at Westminster

share, and to the Party groups in the Chamber of Deputies, which nominated them as their representatives, or even as their delegates, in the Cabinet.

Small wonder that such systems have splintered and dissipated in the face of advancing totalitarianism. His Majesty's Opposition, – a phrase, incidentally, which presupposes the two-Party system – is in fact far too solid to liquidate short of civil war.

Undoubtedly, the concentration of power in the hands of Government presents constitutionalism in Britain with a problem on a scale never before experienced, a problem which, it must be admitted quite frankly, has not yet been solved.

Yet, even here, the method adopted, and particularly the way in which whole industries have been taken over by the State, has been characteristic and peculiar. For the great monopolies, as they have been created, have not been made into Government Departments, like the Post Office. Instead, they have developed like the B.B.C., each vaguely under the general patronage of Government, but under the immediate control of a governing board of its own which is not in practice responsible to Parliament or subject to the control of the Party majority in the House of Commons for matters of day-to-day decision and administration. Each has in practice developed a corporate personality of its own, and the great figures inside each Government monopoly have proved capable of offering public criticism, and even opposition and hostility, to the Government itself.

The great professions have also, in the past, shewn themselves amongst the sources of strength upon which a free community may rely when confronted with tyranny. The legal profession which, it should be remembered, forms three distinct corporations, the Bench, recruited solely from experienced members of the Bar, the Bar itself, and the solicitor's profession, retain not merely absolute autonomy in the control over legal education and admission to the Bar or the Rolls of practising solicitors, but considerable political power.

In the past, British society has shewn an almost unexampled ability to absorb into the Social system new and apparently quite indigestible political and economic theories without marring the underlying harmony and continuity of the life of the community. The Reformation, the Civil War, the Restoration, the Hanoverian Succession, the Reform Bill, Manhood Suffrage, Votes for Women, Puritans, Whigs, Liberals have come and gone. Are we on the way to make a meal of Socialism, digesting the edible matter and excreting the wholly unassimilable, or have we met at last a social and political theory which will bring our society to a full stop, or a wholly new start? Time alone will show, but, on the whole, the evidence appears to be in favour of a new absorption.

This brings me to a discussion of the moral and spiritual characteristics which are supposed to underlie the British, or perhaps I should say the English, capacity for political change, – tolerance, humour, phlegm, and, on the debit side, hypocrisy.

Tolerance in Britain dates about from the time of the Revolution of 1688. Whether it was the result of that revolution, as Macaulay contended, or of bitter weariness of the alternate series of legalised political murders through Parliament during the previous century, must remain in doubt. In Osmond Airy's *Charles II* there is an attractive, if possibly an apocryphal story, which, if it does not give the cause of the change at least illustrates the reason for it.

It seems that during Charles II's reign two drunken peers, Lords Carnarvon and Buckingham, fell into an argument one day as the result of which Carnarvon, who had never previously spoken in the House of Lords, bet Buckingham that he would go there immediately and speak on whatever subject happened to be for debate. It so happened that when they reached the House of Lords they found under discussion a demand from the Commons that Danby, then Lord Treasurer, should be impeached, and committed to prison to await his trial.

Lord Carnarvon, to win his wager, imme-

Above: In the country, the Parish Hall becomes a polling booth on General Election Day. *Below:* At Marble Arch, there is almost unexampled opportunity to absorb – and express – new and quite indigestible political theories

diately rose and made the following maiden speech: 'My Lords,' he said, 'I understand but little of Latin, but a good deal of English and not a little of English history, from which I have learned the mischief of such kinds of prosecutions as these, and the ill fate of the prosecutors. I could bring many instances and those very ancient, but, My Lords, I shall go no further back than the end of Queen Elizabeth's reign about which time the Earl of Essex was run down by Sir Walter Rawleigh. My Lord Bacon, he ran down Sir Walter Rawleigh, – and your Lordships know what became of My Lord Bacon. The Duke of Buckingham, he ran down my Lord Bacon, and your Lordships know what happened to the Duke of Buckingham. Sir Thomas Wentworth, afterwards Earl of Strafford, ran down the Duke of Buckingham, and you well know what became of him. Sir Harry Vane, he ran down the Earl of Strafford, and your Lordships know what became of Sir Harry Vane. Chancellor Hyde, he ran down Sir Harry Vane, and your Lordships know what became of the Chancellor; Sir Thomas Osborne, now Earl of Danby, ran down Chancellor Hyde, but what will become of the Earl of Danby, your Lordships best can tell. But let me see the man that dare run the Earl of Danby down, and we shall see what will become of him.'

As a piece of reasoning on the practical plane this argument proved irresistible. Buckingham's comment: 'The man is inspired, and claret has done the business,' is perhaps an adequate tribute to one of the least appreciated of English political philosophers.

British humour is, perhaps, an older trait. The British have always prided themselves on a kind of understatement, an absence of hyperbole in moments of danger or distress. This is much more the true British humour than the irrepressible facetiousness of the Cockney, with which it is often confused. After all, humour is what it claims to be, a mood rather than an attainment, and a mood having little enough in common with flippancy or even wit. It consists in a certain detachment of mind, showing itself often enough in an ability to smile when others might be wailing or reaching for their six-shooters, but not consisting in any conscious self-restraint so much as an almost Grecian love for moderation and good temper, a desire for the mean in emotion as well as in action, a tendency to pursue a middle path, even when such a course cannot strictly be reconciled with principle or logic. Men of such humour are often accused, and by those who should know better, of an absence of conviction or principle. But moderation is a principle; the philosophy of moderation is a conviction, and a conviction which has worn as well when spun of English worsted or Scottish tweed, as when woven into a cloak for a classical philosopher. If, occasionally, the practice of moderation in all things involves a certain degree of self-deception which others mistake for hypocrisy, if the attempt to rationalize a compromise or a *modus vivendi* involves its defenders in an occasional sophistry, this is no more than to say that, like other virtues, it involves its exponents from time to time in the defects of their qualities. Its consistent pursuit over a period of centuries is to some extent a guarantee of its intellectual integrity, while the dazzling rewards it has heaped upon the nation which has adopted it as a national creed ought, perhaps, to have made it seem worthier of imitation even to its more accomplished critics.

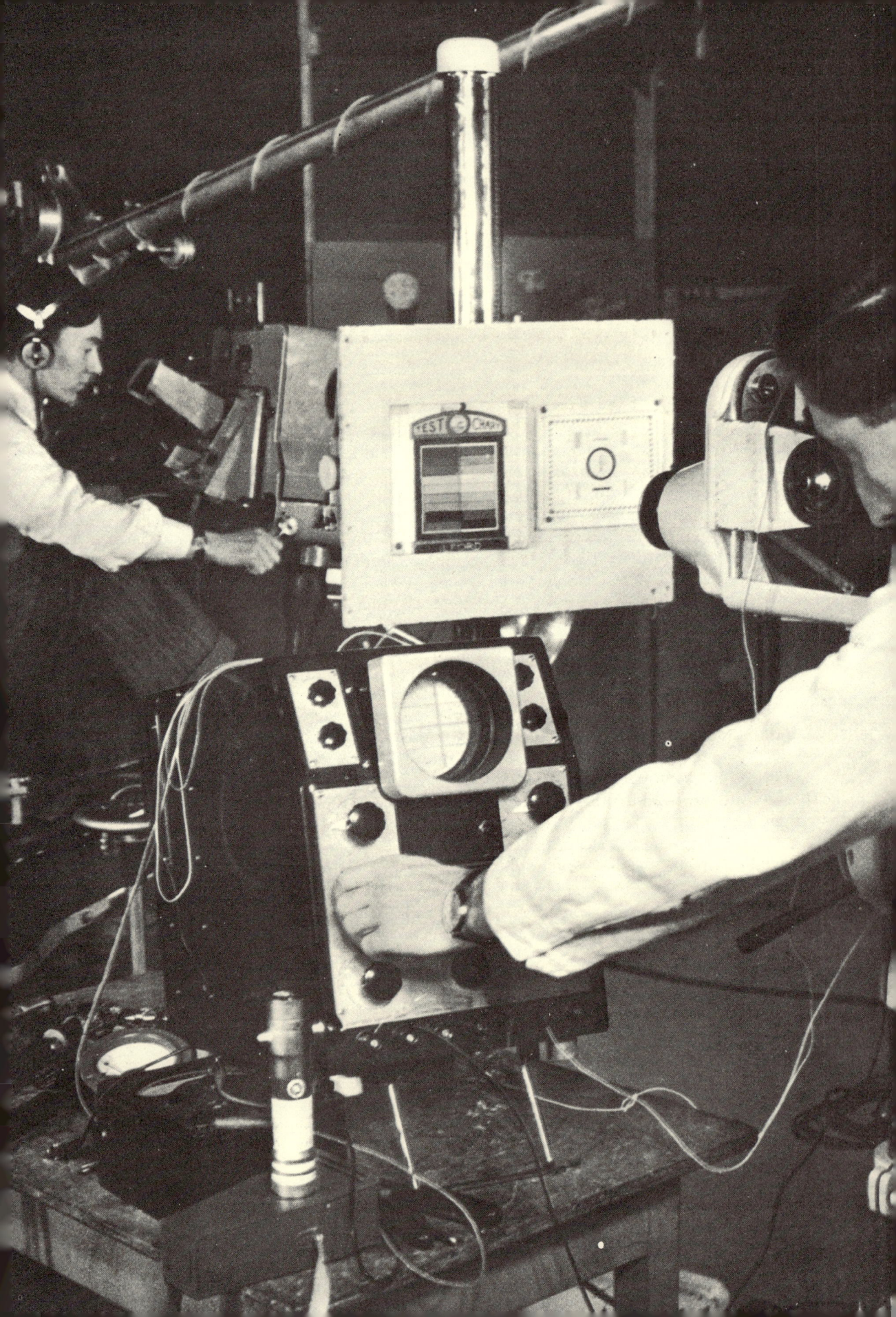

8
THE PRIVATE GENTLEMEN

By Nigel Balchin

During the last war, when British and American scientists were often working side by side, the British found much to admire in American science, and much to envy in its material resources and equipment. But there was one area in which the performance of the young British scientific worker often seemed definitely superior to that of his American opposite number; the area of improvisation – of contriving to produce work of high scientific value under difficult conditions, with a minimum of complicated equipment and facilities. The American was seen at his best when he could bring to bear his superb technical resources; the British scientist when he was forced by the circumstances of war to rely on his personal resourcefulness.

A cynic might say that this was purely a matter of practice – that men accustomed to work in many of the old-fashioned, poorly equipped laboratories that still exist in this country, would have to learn to improvise if they were to work at all effectively. A man who hasn't a battery of calculating machines at his disposal naturally becomes very dexterous with a slide rule. There is some truth in this. But there is another factor that may well have a bearing on the matter – the origins and traditions of British science. That origin, and that tradition, are of the 'amateur' in the best and most accurate sense of the word; not in the sense of 'unskilled' or 'dilettante', but implying the individual who, for sheer love of knowledge, pursues his enquiries, makes his observations, and draws his conclusions from them, finding his true satisfaction in this process itself, rather than in its eventual results from the social or material standpoint.

Francis Bacon, who, with all his faults, was one of the great minds of Elizabethan England, was a man of large ambition. He rose to be a Lord Chancellor of England. He took a prominent part in many of the great events of the day. He fell eventually in disgrace and

Left: Colour Television: first used in Britain as a scientific aid in the teaching hospitals

SIR,

THESE are to give Notice, That on *Monday* the First Day of *December* 1712, (being the next after St. *ANDREW's DAY*) the Council and Officers of the ROYAL SOCIETY are to be Elected for the Year ensuing; at which ELECTION your Presence is expected, at Nine of the Clock in the Forenoon, at the House of the ROYAL SOCIETY, in *Crane Court, Fleet Street.*

To Thomas Isted Esq?

Is. Newton P.R.S.

Above: Summons from a Private Gentleman. *Below:* Frontispiece from Sprat's *History of the Royal Society*, showing Charles II supported by Lord Brounker and Francis Bacon, and a portrait of Newton by Kneller, 1702

John Aubrey, 1626-1697, amateur to end all amateurs, was insatiably interested in absolutely everything

Samuel Pepys, 1633-1703, music-lover, diarist, civil servant, was an early member of the Royal Society

ruin. During this colourful public career he found time to be one of our greatest essayists and thinkers. Yet when we come to read of his death, we find that it was brought about through a chill caught while experimenting with the preservative effects of stuffing a dead bird with snow. Here, four and a half centuries ago, we have the Englishman of many parts, who included amongst them the passionate curiosity to know the how and why of things, and the willingness to go and make experiments to find out. Bacon was a lawyer, a politician, an author. But the last we see of him is as a man with an enquiring mind, catching his death of cold through messing about in the snow with a dead bird, in amateur scientific experiment.

It was only half a century or so later that this typical British passion for scientific knowledge found its most famous expression in the foundation of the Royal Society. Under the patronage of King Charles II, himself a keen amateur scientist with a private laboratory, the Society was founded, and its original ninety-eight Fellows were chosen. It is worth looking at the list of those founder members. There were men like Robert Boyle and Hooke, who were real scientists, in the sense that scientific work was their main preoccupation. But there were also John Dryden, the poet; Christopher Wren, the architect; John Evelyn, the diarist; Charles Stuart, the King; and, amateur to end all amateurs, John Aubrey, who was insatiably interested in absolutely everything from an 'umbrella-like invention for retarding a ship when shee drives in a storm' to a phonetic alphabet, a 'publique banke for the easy raysing of money' and 'the transfusion of Bloud'. Even the Duke of York, later to be the disastrous King James II, was

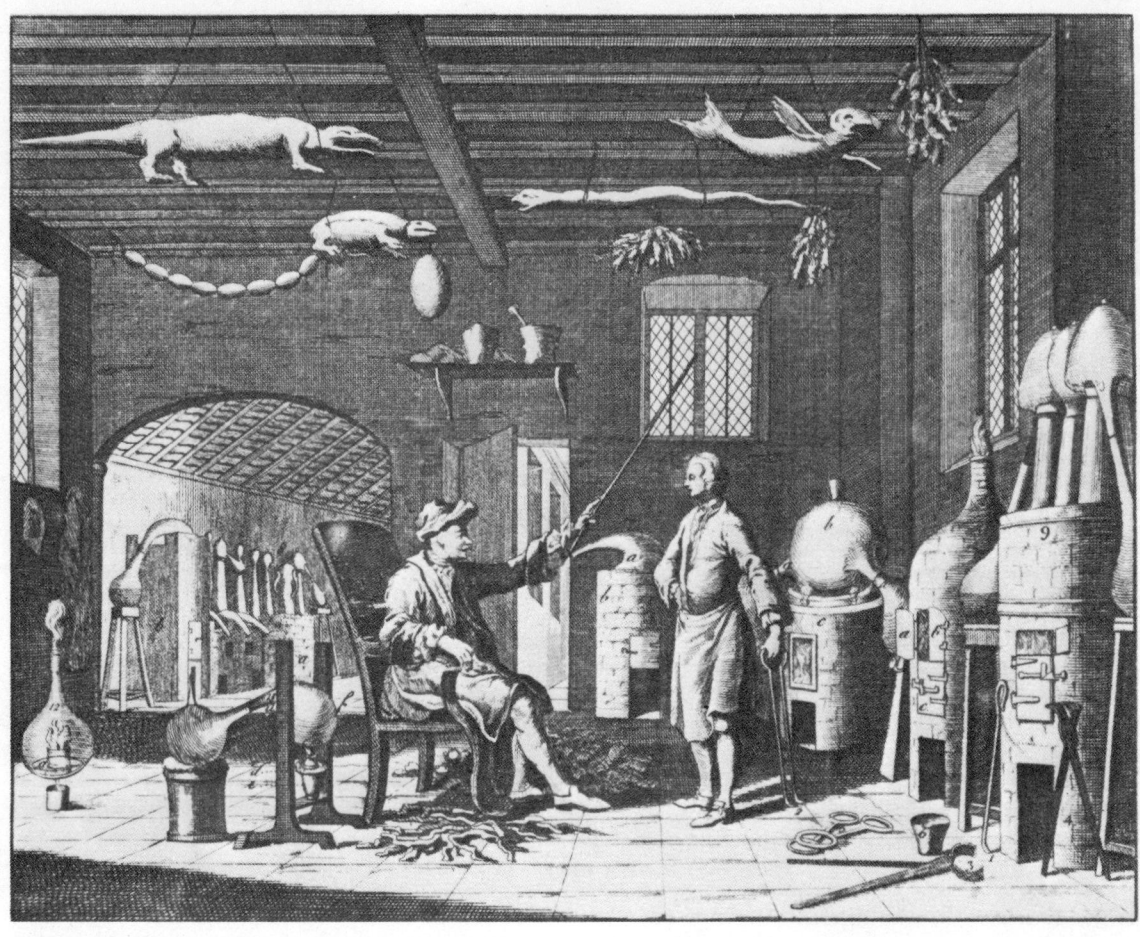

Above: A laboratory in 1789. *Right:* The high tension room of the Cavendish Laboratory, Cambridge

sufficient of a naturalist to discuss, when 'abed with his Duchess at Bath', some unusual snails that he had noticed, and to send for some of them to be collected.

Now the omnivorous amateur of the Aubrey type – the man whose curiosity covers almost the whole field of knowledge – is always trembling on the brink of dilettantism. Indeed, Aubrey himself, like a comic edition of the great Leonardo da Vinci before him, never accomplished as much as lay in his powers, by sheer inability to concentrate his energies. The world of scientific knowledge was already too wide for any man to take it as his parish, and the specialist was the inevitable result. But to specialize is not necessarily to lose the virtues of the true amateur – the curiosity, the individualism, and the sense of the value and pleasure of knowledge for its own sake. Up to a point, Newton specialized. But what could be more superbly amateur than his irritation when pressed to publish the results of some of his most revolutionary work? It had come to something, he said, if a private gentleman could not pursue his enquiries without this constant badgering to make them public. It sounds a curious point of view to us today, when we are accustomed to think of the scientist as the 'servant of the community'. But apart from an amusing antique individualism, Newton may well have been expressing here the scientist's instinctive sense of

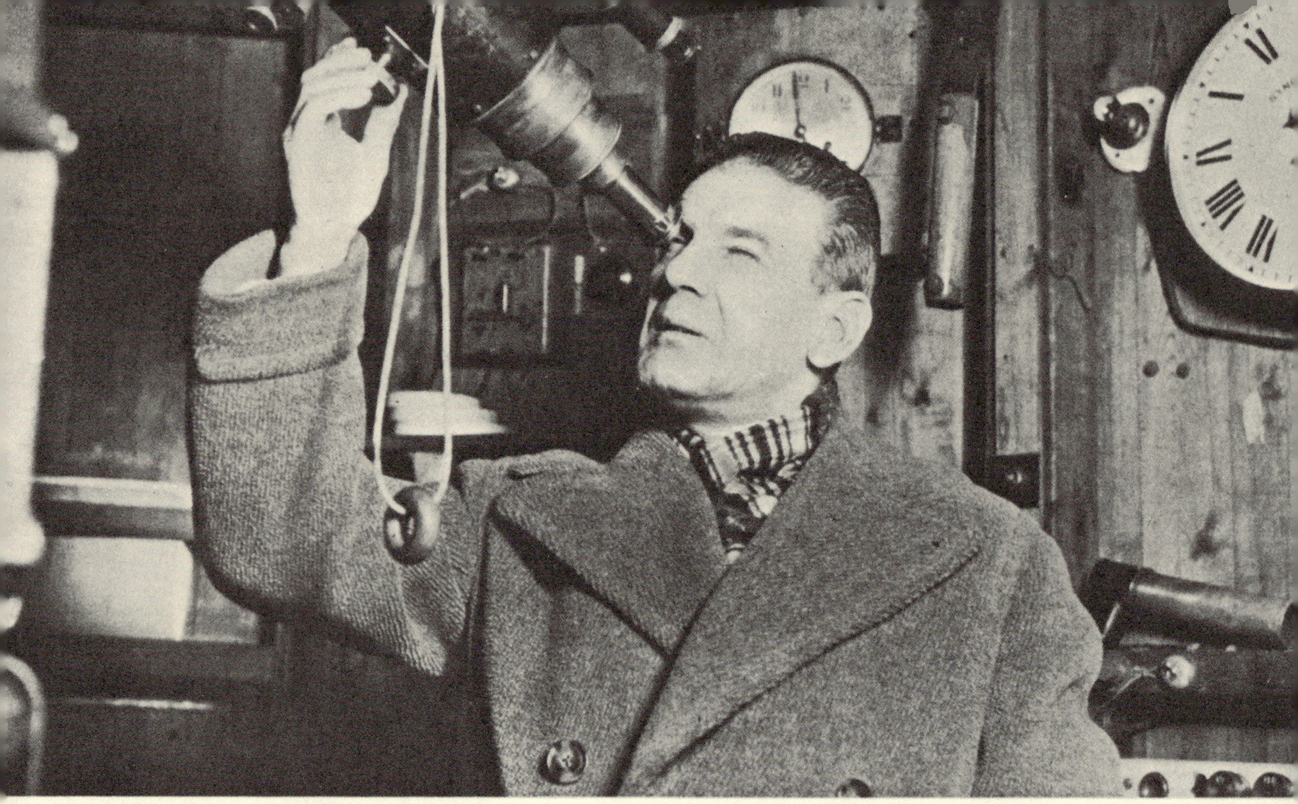

Above: The late Will Hay, in public life a comedian, but privately a serious astronomer. *Below:* An early photograph of Sir John Herschel, 1792-1871, astronomer, photographer, and like Newton, a Master of the Mint

personal, private communication with the truth of the universe – the spirit that animated an eccentric recluse like Cavendish, and would make such men still carry on their researches, even if alone on a desert island without hope of rescue.

It is a far cry from Bacon amusing himself in the snow, and Newton's indignant insistence on his right to privacy, to Faraday and Tyndall and Crookes, and Darwin and Wallace and Huxley. It is not difficult to see why. The Industrial Revolution had vastly increased the purely material potential value of scientific discovery. Had Bacon finished his researches on the preservative use of snow on dead birds, he might or might not have used it to preserve a chicken. But neither he nor anyone else would promptly have made a fortune by founding the refrigerator industry. By the time of the great Victorians, the world was full of gentlemen who were not scientists, and were quite uninterested in the pursuit of knowledge for its own sake, but were acutely interested in the pursuit of it for *their* sake. When Crookes, who had proved his capacity to do something useful and profitable like inventing the miner's lamp, turned his attention to the investigation of survival after death, it was widely and rather indignantly felt that he had no right to waste his time and talents in this way. A more thoroughly 'amateur' enquiry was never undertaken. It did considerable harm to Crookes' reputation as a man and as a scientist. It is difficult to see how it could possibly have done him any material good. In the end, its results were unsatisfactory. Yet here was an issue of immense spiritual importance; and alone, unsupported, Crookes chose, in complete humbleness, to attempt to apply scientific technique to its solution. His reward was to be heartily abused, and told sharply to get on with some useful work. The 'private gentleman' had become the 'servant of the community' – and of its masters. The changed position of the scientist is well illustrated by the famous (and possibly apocryphal) story of Faraday's reply to the statesman who, having been shown some of the early electro-magnetic experiments, asked what *use* it all was? 'Why, sir, there is every possibility that one day you may be able to tax it.' Compared with some of his forerunners, Faraday was a realistic person, who would not have insisted on his 'amateur status' as violently as a Newton. But there is something of Newton's irritation and contempt in that reply – the contempt of the visionary for the over-practical.

And, of course, it is an even further cry from the days of Newton to our own age – the age of J. J. Thompson and Rutherford and Cockcroft and Blackett and Watson-Watt; to Gowland Hopkins and Dodds; to Havelock Ellis; to Whittle; to Crewe and Haldane and Punnett; to Fleming and Flory; to Fisher and Kendall – to all those brilliant scientific horses, known and unknown, who, in the newspaper phrase, have been 'harnessed to the needs of society' in this century. It is not easy to be an amateur in harness. Pulling the social cart is a highly professional job, and one doubts if an Aubrey or a Dryden would now be elected to the Royal Society. The enquiring mind is no longer enough, as anyone can test for himself by attending a discussion of some learned society. Even to take an intelligent interest in a branch of modern science, it is necessary to learn a complete new language. The amateur still exists. The late Will Hay, a well-known comedian who was a serious and capable astronomer in his spare time, was in the true tradition; and one has known B.B.C. officials who were learned botanists, and woollen manufacturers who had private radio laboratories. But there would no longer, one feels, be any amateurs in England's scientific first eleven.

Yet, just as in cricket it is possible to be a professional, and to play with the peculiar zest of the amateur, so in science it is possible to be a learned specialist and yet to retain much of what was good in the 'private gentlemen' of the seventeenth and eighteenth centuries. Indeed, only twenty years ago there was at one of the older Universities a Professor whose general attitude to the publication of his results was not very different from Newton's own. He considered it the least interesting and important part of the job; and the fact that half a dozen of his pupils achieved far greater public recognition than he, on the basis of his work and teaching, left him quite unmoved. If to be a professional is to be serious and skilled and learned, then he was a professional. But if to be an amateur is to be personally and materially disinterested, then he was an amateur.

It is no use to tell men like this that they owe a duty to society, and that they must keep their eye on the material and social ball with all the concentration of a good Civil Servant. That was what the Nazis told their scientists – and nothing contributed more to our winning the war. The scientist has a tremendous social contribution to make. So has the poet. But the contributions of both are mainly indirect – the value to society of the existence within it of a certain type of mind seeking a certain sort of truth; and the more we insist that such a mind shall confine itself to what is directly and obviously and immediately to our benefit, the more we, as society, impoverish our own future.

Modern scientific research is usually an operation carried out by a large and highly organised team, with far more hard, slogging work and far fewer sudden cries of 'Eureka' than is often supposed. But the fact remains that the basic premises from which such work begins, and the drawing of conclusions by which it progresses, are the product of an individual. Nobody would have been more professional than Rutherford, as an organiser and director of team research. Newton, one feels, would not necessarily have been as good a director of the Cavendish Laboratory. But everyone who worked with Rutherford bears witness to the intuitive brilliance of the man's mind – to the fact that, like Newton, he not only had a genius for the discovery and mar-

John Dalton, father of modern chemistry, used these symbols to compare the atomic weight of various elements

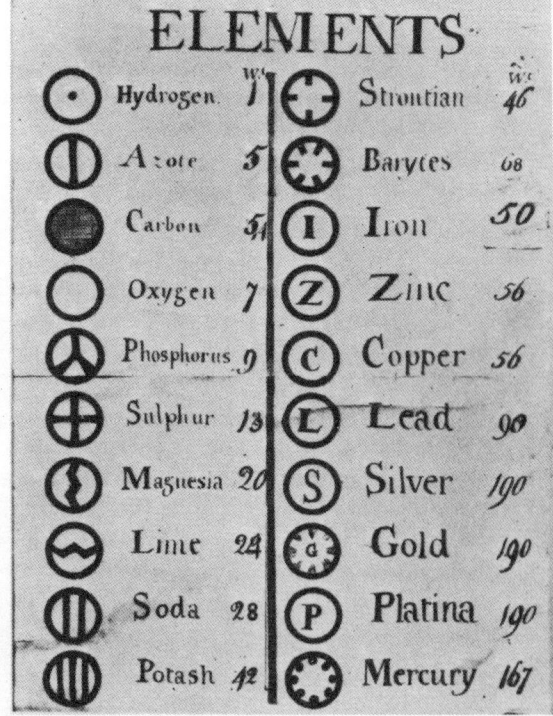

shalling of facts, but for seeing their further implications, and for adding the 'why' of speculation to the 'how' of mere discovery. It would be difficult to find a better example of this capacity for speculation – this instinctive curiosity – than Fleming's discovery of penicillin. A mere laboratory accident – a thing which must have happened thousands of times in laboratories all over the world – gave rise to a chain of speculation, and eventually to a great medical discovery. It is not difficult to see this link here with the first Royal Society. 'Sir Paul Neale sayd', writes Aubrey, 'that in the Bishoprick of Durham is a coalery, which by reason of the dampes ther did so frequently kill the workmen (sometimes three or four in a Moneth) that he could make little or nothing of it. It happened one time, that the workmen being merry with drink fell to play with fire-brands, and to throwe live-coales at one another by the head of the pit, where they usually have fires. It fortuned that a fire-brand fell into the bottome of the Pitt: where at there proceeded such a noise as if it had been a Gun: they likeing the Sport, threw down more fire-brands and there followed the like noise, for severall times, and at length it ceased. They went to work after, and were free from Damps, so having by good chance found out this Experiment, they doe now every morning throw-down some Coales, and they work as securely as in any other Mines.' One can almost write the passage in Aubrey that would have referred to the discovery of penicillin. 'Sir Alexander Fleming, being an ingeniose man, he at work in his laboratory, by chance observed a certain Mould to have appeared. . . .'

No race has excelled the British in producing brilliant experimenters. Yet it seems to me that the truest expression of British scientific genius is in the field of the naturalist-observer and speculator – in the observation of the world with a peculiar type of eye, which

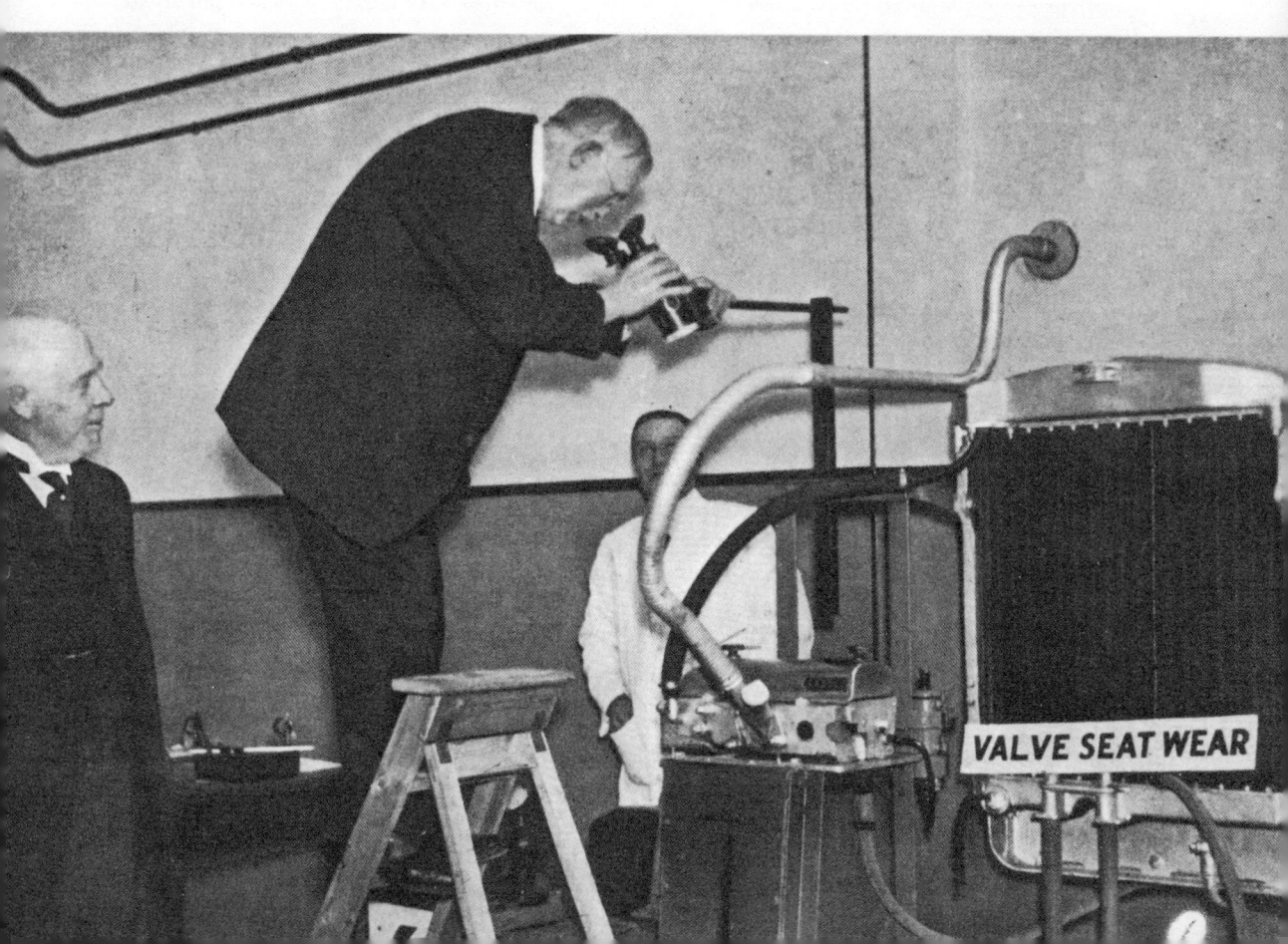

Lord Rutherford's intuitive brilliance added the 'why' of speculation to the 'how' of mere discovery

Above: 'Sir Alexander Fleming, an ingeniose man, he at work, by chance observed a certain Mould ...'
Below: Baird's first television transmission. He once experimented with glass razors and pneumatic socks

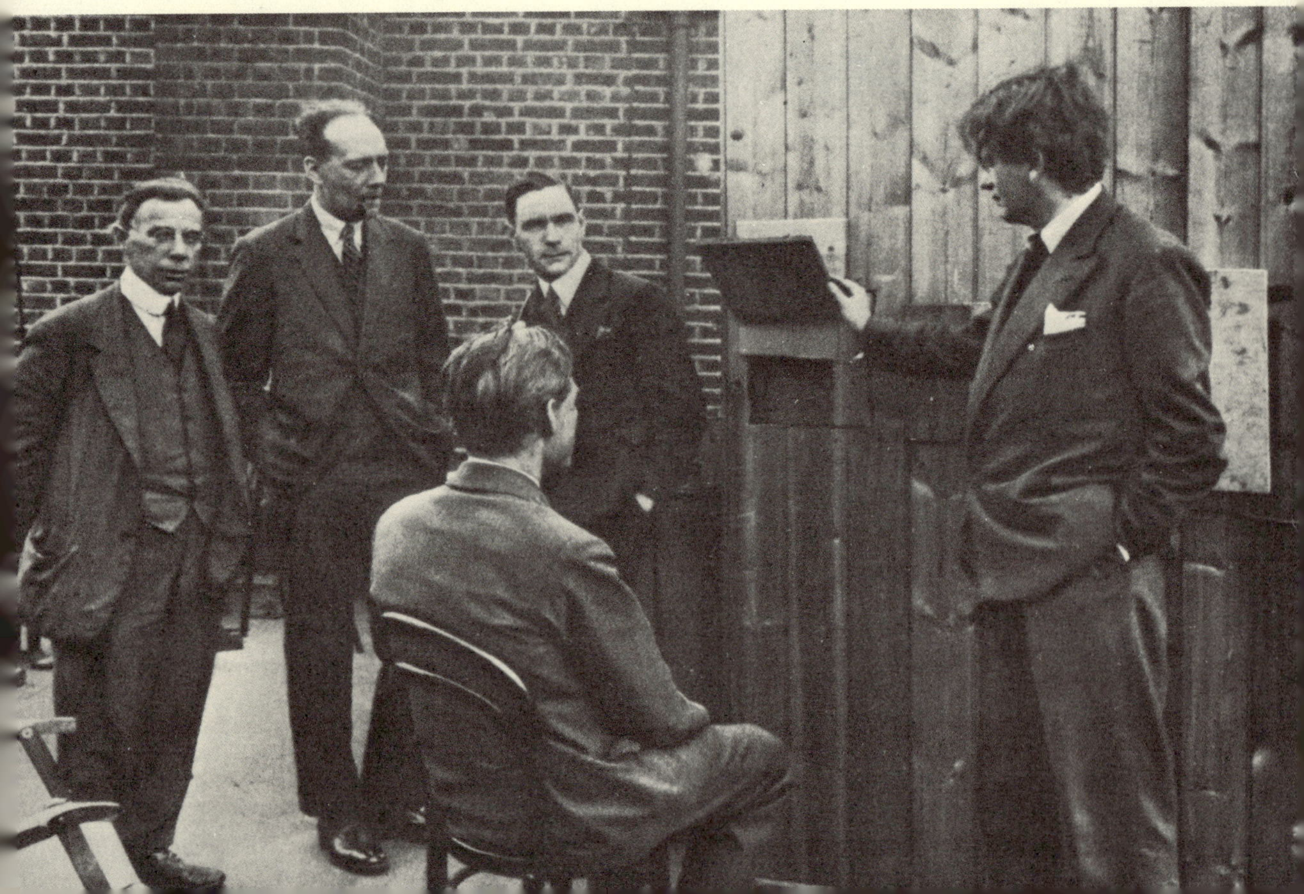

sees through what is there for all to see, to its deeper and more general significance. Sometimes, as in Gilbert White or Havelock Ellis, careful observation and recording are their own justification. Sometimes, as in Darwin's *Origin of Species* or Newton's work on gravitation, observation leads to revolutionary theory. But in either case the work *originates* in a passionate desire to 'use one's eyes' – to look at the natural world, as opposed to giving it a mere passing glance. This is a quality that is less common than we sometimes think – and is perhaps becoming less common in science than it once was. It is not uncommon to find young, highly specialized scientists of vast learning in their own sphere, who are capable of making the most ludicrous mistakes, simply because they are quite uninterested in looking at the world around them, as opposed to the sheet of paper on which they are working. I remember a young research man who, after enormous statistical labour produced some fantastic generalization about the frequency of occurrence of types of human physique. 'But it *must* be so, sir,' he said to a world-famous scientist. 'Look at the figures.' 'No,' was the irritable reply. '*Don't* look at the figures. Go and look at the first six men you meet in the street, and you'll see it's nonsense.'

In a world in which a greater and greater degree of specialization is inevitable, the main danger to science is that workers will cease to be observer-speculators, and become experts in solving a certain specialized type of crossword puzzle, which, as far as they are concerned, has no relationship to life at all. One has only to see a certain type of physicist trying to deal with a psychological problem, or vice-versa, to realize how far both can get from a genuinely scientific attitude when dealing with unaccustomed material.

'Professionalism' has here deteriorated to mean lack of mental scope, or even of interest. Starting from the sound principle of concentrating our vision on some one thing, we have produced an inability to see that thing in its true relationship to anything else. It is here that the great amateur traditions and origins of British science can and do help us. We are often criticized by other nations for a certain absence of fiery effort and enthusiasm. We treat everything, they imply, as though it were a game – a thing done for amusement. Substitute 'for the love of it' and the charge is not one we need worry much about, in science or in any other matter. We can no longer be, like Newton, private gentlemen 'voyaging through strange seas of thought alone.' The best that we can reasonably hope for is to be a Principal Scientific Officer in some vast Government research organization. But at least we can see ourselves not only as Fuel Organic Chemists, or Astro-Physicists, or Plant Pathologists, but as the successors of all the great minds whatever their profession, who have found the universe a matter of wonder and fascination. We are not only the descendants of Hooke and Boyle, but of Dryden also. It was Dryden who once said that to be a good poet a man must have something of the scientist in him. The converse is true; and in the realization that it is true lies much of the greatness of British science.

9
THE GLORY OF THE WORD

By Ivor Brown

That
> The glories of our blood and state
> Are shadows, not substantial things,

is an observation which has been brought to the attention of most students of English literature by now. Why James Shirley's rather gloomy moralising on human transience should be so much quoted I do not know, unless it be for the desire to bring in the haunting final couplet,

> Only the actions of the just
> Smell sweet and blossom in the dust.

This may or may not be a statement of fact, but is certainly consoling to all of us who ever tried to be good.

If analysis of glory be applied to Britain, it is obvious that Shirley's dismissal of 'substantial things' as a basis of national renown is nonsense. The British have been famous for beef and beer and battleships, for boiler-making and suet puddings, for huge bridges and dams, for massive feats of engineering and for country-houses as gigantic as elegant. In shadowy things, to continue with Shirley's phrasing, we have been less notable. We have made sweet music, but never led the world in that. We have painted with grace and force and splendour, but have never mastered the European masters in the galleries any more than we led them in the concert rooms. But there is one art in which the English shadows have danced to perfection, that is in the art of putting thoughts and feelings into words and those words into patterns. For words are the shadows of things.

This English (or British) word-magic is partly due to our old tolerance of immigration. The island was at once a target for invaders and a refuge for escapers. One or the other was always working his way in. Thus the Roman rolled in over the Celt, the Saxon over the Roman, the Norman over the Saxon, and the Renaissance, with its call to a new classicism, swept in over all. Moreover, there was a constant drift into Britain of persecuted peoples, of Jews and Huguenots especially; they brought their brains and their techniques with them and some of their vocabulary also.

Right: Geoffrey Chaucer, *c.* 1340–1400, 'Floure of eloquence, the firste fynder of our faire langage'

Sir Walter Raleigh, poet, courtier, soldier and sailor

The Elizabethan John Bull was anything but beevish

An island, too, is a natural home of sailors and these have continually brought home a cargo of abundant language as well as of rare foods and spices. So the shadowy thing that is a word or a vocabulary was shot through with innumerable colours and given a substance that lifted it far above shadowy status.

Thus it came about that the nation of John Bull, to give it the eighteenth-century symbol for our supposedly gross and beevish selves, has led the world in poetry, especially of the lyrical and fanciful kind, even of the mystical. We have drawn upon so many themes and traditions and also upon so many resources of language, that our writing, both in prose and verse, has had an astonishingly wide range. Because of our habit of accepting and absorbing we have had all the best literatures of the world and all their best words at our disposal and the national genius for assimilation and for compromise – that genius is a fact as well as a cliché – has received and digested and turned into nerve and brain this double supply of native and imported thought and language.

That stockish, stupid figure of John Bull, all chin and no brain, bone from the neck upwards, a masculine oaf both paunchy and pugilistic, has terribly misled the world. The English have been a mixed and a mysterious people since the Romans came, far more mixed and mysterious when we got the second and bloodless Roman invasion, which was the Renaissance. Shakespeare's London was full of 'fantasticoes' – lisping of foreign arts, cutting foreign capers in the dance, importing the notions of 'ingenious Italy' and brandishing foreign words along with their swords. It swarmed also with much-travelled veterans of the wars and exploration, and so it was much more like a European capital than an English country town. Its noblemen were the greatest amateurs of all time, now soldiering, now courting, now sailoring, now sonneteering, now brawling, now singing, men with the lutes of love as well as the steel of contention in their hands.

They were intensely musical and every man was expected to have enough harmony in his soul to take his part in a madrigal. During Shakespeare's time one of the prominent English musicians was actually called John Bull and it is interesting to discover from his portrait that he was no red-necked mass of blood and brawn, but a slim, dark Italianate creature who might have been as native to Milan as to Westminster. I take that man to be a significant type of Elizabeth's England, in which to be musical was to be normal, to write poetry was a practice proper to a gentleman, and have the airs, graces and lingo of Continental fashion was the natural product of the European journeys in which all who could afford it indulged during their young manhood.

Small wonder, then, that the English language flourished in such a period of expansion and importation. It had the stout Saxon monosyllables on which to build; it had the classical polysyllables with which to adorn and to fortify. So the poets could vary a sounding eloquence with a poignant brevity, a feat in which Shakespeare especially excelled. Let us take two passages from *King Lear* to exemplify the double process. A storm demands linguistic rumblings and verbal bastinado – and gets it.

Blow, winds, and crack your cheeks! rage! blow!
You cataracts and hurricanoes, spout
Till you have drench'd our steeples, drown'd the cocks:
You sulphurous and thought-executing fires,
Vaunt-couriers to oak-cleaving thunderbolts,
Singe my white head! And thou, all-shaking thunder,
Strike flat the thick rotundity o' the world,
Crack nature's moulds, all germens spill at once,
That make ingrateful man!

Of this word-deluge, so appropriate to the scene, cataracts are Greek, hurricanoes blew in from the Spanish Main, vaunt-couriers are French and rotundity and germens Latin. Now contrast this with Lear's dying words.

And my poor fool is hang'd! No, no, no life,
Why should a dog, a horse, a rat, have life,
And thou no breath at all? Thou'lt come no more,
Never, never, never, never, never, –
Pray you, undo this button: thank you, sir.
Do you see this? Look on her – look, her lips –
Look there, look there! –

That reads flatly enough: yet on the stage, and well acted, it can be unbearably tragic. Except for the repeated 'never' and the 'button' the passage is purely monosyllabic and mainly Anglo-Saxon in its word-formation. When Shakespeare drove at pathos, he knew exactly how to choose the short, the simple, and the stabbing word. In this blending of the tiny and the tremendous he was assisted by the hospitality of the English language which had accepted its word for storm from Scandinavia and its hurricanoes from the Caribbean. It was constantly increasing both its picturesque and its musical quality by holding on to the strange and sounding terms which its soldiers and sailors of fortune brought home.

If we turn to our own time, we find another superb master of English, Mr. Winston Churchill, mixing the rolling period with a string of single syllables. When writing of old age and the practice of painting as a mitigation of its pains he alludes to 'the surly advance of decrepitude', not to the oncoming of old age. When he is talking of the great deeds of war he can say, with a brevity that will outlive all eloquence, 'Never was so much owed by so many to so few'. He knows, as Shakespeare knew, how to ring the changes between an orchestrated Latinity and the quiet tolling of a Saxon bell.

No sooner had I written that last sentence, with its allusion to a bell, than I discovered that I was becoming a plagiarist. Reading Miss C. V. Wedgwood's admirable contribution to the Home University Library on *Seventeenth Century Literature*, I found her citing an old argument between Thomas Campion and Sir John Beaumont. Campion had pleaded for a rich flow of words in the Renaissance manner, since 'the concourse of our monosyllables makes our verses unapt to slide'. To which Beaumont replied in rhyme:

Our Saxon shortness hath peculiar grace
In choice of words fit for the ending place,
Which leave impression in the mind as well
As closing sounds of some delightful bell.

Of course both pleaders had right on their side. The evocative power of the English language has been sustained by its balance of trade between the gaudy and the unassuming native goods. Shakespeare, in one of his earliest

and most richly worded plays *Love's Labour's Lost* made this point, when his precious and garrulous character Berowne determined to lay aside for a while his 'taffeta phrases, silken terms precise' and replace them with his 'russet yeas and honest kersey noes' – kersey being a strong, coarse cloth named after a village in Suffolk. The English tongue, when it was cloyed with foreign meats, could always return to, and profit by, the native bread and cheese.

One aspect of linguistic history is easily overlooked; it was really much easier to write well in Elizabeth's reign than it is now. The words, whether aboriginal or exotic, were all comparatively fresh: they had not been frayed and dented by excessive and continual usage. Here, in Shakespeare's own phrase, was this great 'alms-basket of words' with the countryside sending its own vocabulary up to London and London sending its foreign acquisitions back into the country. The writers' invention added to the store which was as unsullied as a posy of garden-flowers. Nowadays all our words are fatigued and the sort of term that meant something tremendous to Shakespeare, e.g. thrill, for a shudder down the back, has been so battered by usage that we hardly notice it. 'My dear, I'm thrilled!' It means almost nothing on the lips of a girl of to-day. But when Shakespeare wrote of 'thrilling regions of thick-ribbèd ice' he conveyed to his audience all the fearsomeness of a polar winter.

The translators of the Authorised Version of the Bible had a young, plastic, lively speech on which to work. So many of their phrases have become commonplace owing to continual (and now almost unconscious) repetition that we fail to realise how beautiful they are. The Book of Common Prayer is one of the greatest poems in the English language, but much mumbling and intoning and routine delivery have dulled our ears to its beauty. Inevitably, as times roll on and the volumes of written stuff accumulate by the million, it is harder than ever to coin a new phrase or to forge a new simile or metaphor. Shakespeare and the men of his period 'got in on the ground floor', as they say of financial matters.

Above: Shakespeare's tomb in Stratford Church
Left: 'Blow winds, and crack your cheeks! rage! blow!' The storm scene in Royston Morley's television production of *King Lear*. William Devlin as Lear, Robert Sansom as Kent, and Alan Wheatley as the Fool

'Never was so much owed by so many to so few.' Churchill's brief words that will outlive all eloquence

The English way of writing began to stiffen and grow formal in the seventeenth and eighteenth centuries when classicism was the governing influence. Milton was, in a way, the English voice of Virgil emerging from a Puritan cassock and Dryden and Pope, whose minds if not their bodies wore the toga, both regarded simplicity as barbarous; study was essential, study of the ancient laws and models of elegant composition.

>True ease in writing comes from art, not chance,
>As those move easiest who have learned to dance.

But those who had not mastered the academic steps and could not join in the minuet of phraseology were determined to state the other case. In a century's time there was an inevitable reaction against the allegiance to Latinity and to an artificial language of supposed fancy, the sort of lingo in which love was always spoken of in the same set terms; suitors of fair hands prated of their fancy, rapture, flame, Cupid's darts and so forth. In Scotland short-lived Fergusson, followed by Robert Burns who lived just long enough to make his name immortal, were drawing upon the native Scottish speech in order to re-establish the simplicities of phrase and feeling. When the latter said that his love was like a red, red, rose that's newly sprung in June, he declared no original sentiment, but, by escaping from celestial raptures and all the ceremonial stuff about Venus and the arrows of Eros, he had tidied away a lot of withered flowers which were cumbering the workshop of the language and the minds of the poets.

In England Wordsworth did very much the same, declaring that poetry is the spontaneous overflow of powerful feelings and not a calculated product. Poetry, he argued, therefore requires spontaneity of speech, the natural idiom and the vocabulary of the ordinary man. The result need not be flat, because the poet's feeling can raise language to a higher power.

>Sensations sweet
>Felt in the blood and felt along the heart

demand their own appropriate expression.

And Wordsworth in English, as Burns in his own Scots, could provide that expression. They purified, one might even say they glorified, the language of poetry by deflating it. Such a quatrain as

> She lived unknown and few could know
>   When Lucy ceased to be;
> But she is in her grave, and Oh,
>   The difference to me.

is almost banal. And yet it is somehow moving, certainly more moving than if the grave had been called a sepulchre and Lucy had been wrapped in 'cerements' in the grand manner of Shakespeare's cemetery-rhetoric. Take the lines before that:

> She dwelt among the untrodden ways
>   Beside the springs of Dove,
> A maid whom there were none to praise
>   And very few to love.

How would an earlier poet have rendered that? Perhaps in this way:

> In solitude's sweet unsequestered ways
>   Beside th' emerging founts of plashing Dove,
> Unsung by swains' encomiastic lays
>   She lived, unpierced by darting wounds of love.

That I think is not unfair to the more frigid hands that worked in the Augustan school. Which has the greater glory of the word? Wordsworth, of course, simply by denying himself words.

But there is always a pendulum in any language and the swing of it carried the Victorians back into the search for a sonorous vocabulary. This swing reached its summit in the rich, melodious, and sometimes almost meaningless eloquence of Swinburne. His political and unethical audacities, in an age of strict moral discipline and censorship, as well as his extraordinary command of rhyme and rhythm, made him so much the adored champion of insurgent youth in the eighteen-sixties that the undergraduates of Cambridge are said to have linked arms and chanted his choruses on King's Parade. Here was glory of the word indeed!

Swinburne hymning 'The lilies and languors of virtue' and 'the raptures and roses of vice' was a constant explorer of 'alliteration's artful aid'. But so, in various ways, are all adroit users of words. It is one of the most

Roosevelt – 'Rhetoric into eloquence would not go'

serviceable features of the English language that playing on sounds and letters, by emphasising them, repeating them, or alternating them, can have direct and subtle emotional effects. This is a fact which all our masters of prose and poetry have discovered and exploited. 'Glory of orator, glory of song,' wrote Tennyson and in a way, his own poetry combined them both.

Very obvious alliteration can be tiresome. Tennyson's

> The moan of doves in immemorial elms
> And murmur of innumerable bees

is almost too much. So are these lines of Swinburne's,

> For winter's ruins and rains are over
> And all the season of snows and sins.

The author of 'Atalanta in Calydon' could run on like that for ever, not pausing to think over the implications. (Why is winter more sinful than summer? If it had suited him Swinburne would have written 'And all the season of sun and sin'.)

But the intertwining of letter-effects, as practised, perhaps unconsciously and intuitively, by Shakespeare, can have great poignancy and potency. In one after another of his most famous passages we can note the intricate patterning of his letter-play. The dying Cleopatra begins her noble farewell thus,

> Give me my robe, put on my crown: I have Immortal longings in me: Now no more –

The alliteration there is not of initial letters, which is the obvious way of playing the trick. It consists of the repeated letter 'o' inside the words employed, coupled with the roll of the 'r' in robe, crown, immortal, and more.

It is an easily noted fact that the letter 'r' is of great emotional value to English poets and that a word containing it, especially if linked with the letter 'o' or a long 'a', can be of powerful assistance to them. Why, for example, does the word rose seem so much more beautiful than lily, why does it drop so surely on the heart? Simply because of its fortunate lettering. Why should 'farewell' be so much more moving a word than 'goodbye'? There is something in the sound of it, you say, and, when you begin to analyse the sound, you find that words with long 'a's and 'o's assisted by 'r's are usually of supreme value in driving at the feelings. Why is war a compelling word while strife is not? Why is glamour, albeit a word now dreadfully overworked, so much more bewitching than magic? Why is grief more touching than pain? Why is to abhor more terrible than to hate? Study of the unconscious reactions to special letters and syllables is fascinating: one thing it consistently proves, namely the wealth of sound-values which our composite English language, with its amalgam of native growths and imports, so fortunately contains.

How then does this English language stand at the present time? It has a splendid inheritance, but, as I said, words do wear out, so that terms which had tremendous associations and potency three hundred years ago now seem only commonplace. Awful is another example of this; once suggesting total horror it is now only a synonym for nasty. Moreover we have lost interest in eloquence and rhetoric. Public speaking used to be an important element in public life and the swaying of an audience by copious and compelling words was an art which the young gentlemen intending, as most young gentlemen did, to be statesmen, had to study.

But circumstances have altered all that. As democracies grow bigger and bigger the direct verbal approach to one single audience gathered in one meeting-place becomes less and less effective in a political campaign. Modern inventions have enabled the politician to shout at his constituents with loud-speakers and to approach the entire nation by way of the microphone. Indeed the microphone is increasingly used for debates and addresses on every kind of topic.

This, one might have thought, would greatly increase the scope of rhetoric and the art of word-usage and so enrich the language with new rhythms of the orator and with an appealing and expanding vocabulary. But exactly the opposite occurred. It was discovered that rhetoric into broadcasting will not go. Carefully compiled paragraphs sound false and affected when spoken into the microphone. The victorious broadcaster has to possess a conversational tone and fireside manner which persuade the myriads of dispersed listeners that the Great Man is talking personally and intimately to them in their own homes. Only the vocabulary of common use and wont can be employed. Therefore the microphone, instead of adding to our glory of words, has undoubtedly diminished it. This is not only the century of the Ordinary Man; it is the century of the Ordinary Word.

That has been noticeable in the theatre which once depended largely on the majesty of the English language expressed in high Tudor poetry or on Restoration Comedy or on the rich fustian of melodrama. But the coming of realism, that is to say of plain-clothes plays about workaday problems written in the prose that we all use in our casual conversation, has diminished the language, in just the same way that broadcasting has pared away instead of

Above: A scene from *The Lady's not for Burning*. Fry is a hopeful poet who delights in the handsomeness of words
Below : Hope in a Runyon movie. America leads the English-speaking union in forging the pungent phrase

T. S. Eliot, a leader in the revival of the poetic play

enlarging verbal richness. Few dramatists, for example, have used a more sparse vocabulary than Noel Coward. Very amusing and incisive he can be, but if he is the Sheridan of our day, then Sheridan has lost his voice. Coward's characters have been described as talking like typewriters and what they chiefly tap out is a metallic click of monosyllables.

Shaw, on the other hand, because he was never an authentic realist and was ready to make most of his characters talk with all his force and fluency, did maintain a species of rhetoric, finely phrased and built up into imposing word-structures, and so he preserved for us in our modern theatre some at least of the old glory of words. I would particularly cite the beginning and end of *Back to Methuselah* and the Trial Scene in *St. Joan* as examples of Shavian prose, at once ample and exact, 'proper words in proper places', to use the definition of style made by his fellow Irishman and master of English, Swift.

Fortunately there has been a revival of poetic play-writing with T. S. Eliot and Christopher Fry as leaders. Eliot himself has never much affected a poet's traditional vocabulary and he generally writes his poetical plays with a spareness and a bareness of language which are not far removed from that of naturalistic prose. Often he gives us conversational English, cut to verse-patterns. Fry, however, is frankly and happily a word-spinner, one who delights in the glimmer of a phrase, the delivery of a far-flung fancy, and in juggling with nouns and adjectives that are bright as new-painted toys. No sooner has the curtain gone up on Fry's *The Lady's not for Burning* than a young woman speaks like this.

Coming in from the light, I am all out at the eyes.
Such white doves were paddling in the sunshine
And the trees were as bright as a shower of broken
  glass.
Out there, in the sparkling air, the sun and the rain
Clash together like the cymbals clashing
When David did his dance. I've an April blindness.
You're hidden in a cloud of crimson catherine-
  wheels.

and a man says later:

                                          I can see
The sky's pale belly glowing and growing big,
Soon to deliver the moon. And I can see
A glittering smear, the snail-trail of the sun
Where it crawled with its golden shell into the hills.

and in his following play *Venus Observed* he has some superb landscape, e.g.:

If you could have seen in your embryonic eye
The realm of bryony, sloes, rose-hips,
And a hedge's ruin, a golden desuetude,
A countryside like a drowned angel
Lying in shallow water, every thorn
Tendering a tear.

I think the success of Fry's plays a most significant pointer, because so many poets of recent years have been uninterested in the melody and the handsomeness of words: they dealt in speculation rather than emotion and in the twisted expression of their own complicated doubts and frustrations. There might be subtlety of reflection that way, but there could hardly be grandeur of speech. But Fry has reclaimed the stage for the eye of fancy and for the tongue that embodies fancy in sonorous and decorated sentences. He has something of the Elizabethan joy in a good loud shout of glee: he sings at his desk, as others in their bath. If more follow him we shall escape the chattery-smattery prose of the realistic comedy with its lounge-hall setting and its trivial antics of sexual manoeuvre. In the winter of 1950 he carried his conquests further and was tumultuously acclaimed in New York.

At the same time there are other inventors at work on many levels of life. There are the advertisers who have to find unfamiliar words for the salesmanship of very familiar articles and so must be ceaselessly fruitful in adjectives and metaphors. There are the journalists continually striving to abbreviate words for the sake of space and heighten them for the sake of force. Above all, there is slang, both native and imported. Slang is often a form of poor man's or 'tough guy's' poetry, as when an American toper says that he has been 'high as a kite', since such was the elevating power of his inebriation. It cannot be denied that America leads the English-Speaking union in its power to forge new vernacular phrases, vivid, pungent, and picturesque. With its amalgam of inflowing races it has been on a vast scale, what Shakespeare's England was on a small one, a melting-pot of language as of people. Moreover, it has retained with their original meanings many of the words which the Pilgrim Fathers took as part of their mental luggage on that astounding adventure of theirs. When an American calls the pavement the side-walk he is talking Pilgrim-Father-wise and using an English seventeenth-century term; incidentally, it happens to be more suitable than our own since any part of the road can be paved, while the name side-walk explains exactly what the thing is. It is often said that the best pronunciation of English occurs in Inverness: it can fairly be added that some of the best English vocabulary has remained and enriched itself in New England.

In conclusion, I think that our poetry has worked through its lean years, when the young writers, wearied, with some justice, of the too mellifluous routine of post-Tennysonian composition and the hearty songfulness of the Georgians, forswore the beautiful and the sensuous and concentrated, like their colleagues of the studio, on the stark and the distorted. We have had Picassian poetry as well as Cubism and Surrealism and all the other strident and contentious -Isms of the canvas. All schools in the arts are, rightly as well as naturally, transient, if not ephemeral. We are volatile in our language as in our habits. The reaction to a style less jejeune and austere has already begun; may it continue!

The LAWS of the NOBLE GAME of CRICKET
as Established at the Star and Garter Pall Mall by a Committee of Noblemen & Gentlemen

THE BALL
Must not weigh less than five Ounces and a half, nor more than five Ounces and three Quarters.

It cannot be changed during the Game, but with Consent of both Parties.

THE BAT.
Must not exceed Four Inches and One Quarter in the widest Part.

THE STUMPS
Must be Twenty two Inches the Ball Six Inches long.

N.B. It is lately settled to use three Stumps instead of two to each Wicket, the Ball the same Length as above.

THE BOWLING CREASE
Must be parallel with the Stumps Three Feet in Length with a Return Crease.

THE POPPING CREASE.
Must be Three Feet Ten Inches from the Wickets, and the Wickets must be opposite to each other, at the Distance of Twenty two Yards.

THE PARTY,
which goes from home,

Shall have the choice of the Innings, and the pitching of the Wickets, which shall be pitched within Thirty Yards of a Centre fixed by the Adversaries.

When the Parties meet at a Third Place, the Bowlers shall toss up for the pitching of the First Wicket, and the Choice of going in.

THE BOWLER.
Must deliver the Ball with one Foot behind the Bowling Crease, and within the Return Crease, and shall bowl four Balls before he changes Wickets, which he shall do but once in the same Innings.

He may order the Player at his Wicket to stand on which Side of it he pleases.

THE STRIKER,
is out

If the Ball be bowled off, or the Stump bowled out of the Ground —

Or if the Ball from a stroke over or under his Bat or upon his Hands (but not Wrists) is held before it touches the Ground though it be hugged to the Body of the Catcher —

Or if in striking, both his Feet are over the Popping Crease, and his Wicket is put down, except his Bat is grounded within it —

Or if the runs out of his Ground to hinder a Catch —

Or if the Ball is struck up, and he wilfully strikes it again —

Or if in running a Notch the Wicket is struck down by a Throw, or with the Ball in Hand before his Foot, Hand or Bat is grounded over the Popping Crease, but if the Ball is off a Stump must be struck out of the Ground by the Ball.

Or if the Striker touches or takes up the Ball before it has lain still, unless at the Request of the Opposite Party.

Or if the Striker puts his Legs before the Wicket, with a Design to stop the Ball, and actually prevents the Ball from hitting the Wicket by it.

If the Players have crossed each other, he that runs for the Wicket that is put down is out, if they are not crossed, he that has left the Wicket that is put down is out.

When the Ball has been in the Bowler's or Wicket Keeper's Hands, the Strikers need not keep within their Ground, till the Umpire has called Play, but if the Player goes out of his Ground with an Intent to run before the Ball is delivered the Bowler may put him out.

When the Ball is struck up in the Runway Ground between the Wickets, it is lawful for the Strikers to hinder its being catched, but they must neither strike at, nor touch the Ball with their Hands.

If the Ball is struck up, the Striker may guard his Wicket either with his Bat or his Body.

In Single Wicket Matches, if the Striker moves out of the Ground to strike at the Ball, he shall be allowed no Notch for such Stroke.

The WICKET KEEPER
Shall stand at a reasonable Distance behind the Wicket and shall not move till the Ball is out of the Bowler's Hand and shall not by any Noise incommode the Striker, and if his Hands, Knees, Foot or Head be over or before the Wicket, though the Ball touch it, it shall not be out.

THE UMPIRES
Shall allow Two Minutes for each Man to come in, and Fifteen Minutes between each Innings, when the Umpire shall call Play the Party refusing to play, shall lose the Match.

They are the sole Judges of fair and unfair Play, and all Disputes shall be determined by them.

When a Striker is hurt they are to allow another to come in, and the Person hurt shall have his Hands in any Part of that Innings.

They are not to order a Player out, unless appealed to by the Adversaries. — But if the Bowler's Foot is not behind the Bowling Crease, & within the Return Crease, when he delivers the Ball, the Umpire unasked must call No Ball.

If the Strikers run a short Notch, the Umpires must call No Notch.

BETS
If the Notches of one Player are laid against another, the Headsponds on both Innings, unless otherwise specified.

If one Party beats the other in one Innings, the Notches in the First Innings shall determine the Bet.

But if the other Party goes in a second Time, then the Bet must be determined by the Numbers on the Score

THE END.

10
THE FANATICS

By Stephen Potter

Dear Stranger, you are visiting Britain for the first time, in 1951. You have heard that Britain is fanatical about games, fanatically proud of her games and sports, fanatically convinced that games began in this island and that we have taught the rest of the world how to play them, fanatically sure that, though by dosing themselves with patent foods, training themselves by lifting weights or driving golf-balls off the deck of the *Queen Mary*, sneaking unfair advantages by using more tightly strung rackets or shorter shorts, foreign players may sometimes beat us, these defeats represent a momentary dip, only, of fortune's wheel.

You are told moreover that however casual we may be about bombs, war, Westminster Abbey, and Shakespeare, the British are fanatics for games.

You want in other words to understand Britain better by understanding her games-mindedness.

There is, I believe, a key and an explanation to this problem. But when, Stranger, you first begin to study the British games-player you will be bewildered without some kind of Guide to our British games Characters.

These we will now proceed to analyse. This is our Guide.

First, the anti-gamesplayer. The visitor must understand that in Britain games are right, good, 'O.K.' It is right to be fond of games, good at games, bad at games but a tryer and a 'good loser', interested in watching games if you can't play them, knowledgeable about games, hard-workingly a reader of games history, lore, and fact.

To certain English types, however, games are silly. Totally misunderstanding what we will see to be the basic character of English sport, they regard games as childish and a waste of time. Besides certain doctors and artists who do actually seem to be too busy to play games, there are philosophers and analysts (who know too much about the sublimation involved) to be able to take part themselves. Francophiles and slavish admirers of

Left: 'A bumping pitch and a blinding light – an hour to play and the last man in.' *Newbolt*

The British are fanatically convinced that defeats represent a momentary dip only in fortune's wheel. *Above:* Miss G. Moran at Wimbledon. *Below:* Britons created the backhand half volley and the underhand twist service

Major Wingfield's game, 'sphairistike', patented by him in 1874. He thus *invented* modern lawn tennis

the Gallic way of life rightly believe that the English attitude to games is un-French.

True British gamesplayers may be subdivided into the following Seven Types. First the man who mixes up games with the apparatus for keeping fit. He wakes up in the morning and examines his skin carefully. He sees 'a small red patch or dot on his cheek,' he says, 'My God'; he adds, 'A slight paralysis of the capillaries. I must reorganise my life. This is the effect of drink.' Later he tells his friend that he has a minute hangover.

FRIEND: So have I and it's not completely minute. I'm going to have a Turkish bath.
FITMAN: Good, but no good for me. It just gives me a headache.
FRIEND: Sweat it clean away –
FITMAN: Precisely what I am going to do, but from within outwards by playing squash at the Lansdowne. I'll get Deans to give me a work-out. He stands stock still in the centre of the court – while I rush round trying to retrieve. If I put on two sweaters I shall feel marvellous, twenty minutes after. That feeling after getting out of the bath . . . the feeling of lightness, all refuse shed, feeling the shape of your own legs – arms and legs seem to belong to you once more. . . .

But the fit man can't exist by squash alone. Fresh air, open air, must blow in as well.

'I smoked sixty cigarettes yesterday. I often do when I'm actually in the Works . . . I shall play golf tomorrow on the upper course at Moor Park – there's always plenty of air and light there . . . I shall have one cigarette on the first tee, one on the tenth, and perhaps one more at the final key hole. . . .'

Later the exercise has made him hungry.

'Fool that I am!' he says. 'Too many potatoes. I feel sleepy, stupefied. I shall just slip round to Wilson's and suggest a short sharp game of snooker. Played briskly, it works off the feeling of food very well, really.'

At this point he bends at right angles and goes through the motions of cueing.

TYPE TWO is quite different. Type Two is the 'I saw Rexgrove' man. We will call him 'Carthusian'. Carthusian last saw Rexgrove thirty-three years ago, at school at Charterhouse. But when he went off to see Oxford play Cambridge at hockey, he saw Rexgrove.

'Rather extraordinary, there were two Charterhouse people playing for Oxford.'

It is also rather strange that there was an old Carthusian, Pope, in the train, playing gin rummy on an old macintosh stretched between his knees and the knees of the man opposite who wasn't, as far as he knew, an old Carthusian himself.

But the extraordinary thing was that Rexgrove was having a drink in the Committee Bar, spotted Carthusian, and asked him to come in and he, Carthusian, actually had this drink in the Committee Bar. Carthusian began to be not so sure he hadn't seen Waddington, in shorts, acting as linesman. Waddington came to Charterhouse the year he left, in 1922.

TYPE THREE is the Text-Book. He special-

Casual we may be about bombs, Westminster Abbey and Shakespeare, but the darts tournament is a serious affair

ises in theory, believes that his game can be improved by study, has slow motion cinema films taken of his back-hand shot at lawn-tennis, and has pinned to his wall enlarged photographs of hands gripping rackets, diagrams of the trajectory of darts, and open by his bed a shiny pamphlet called *Essential Bowls*. The most remarkable characteristic of this man's gamesplay is that he never seems to be engaged in an actual match but always preparing for one. He will place a cricket cap in the corner of a lawn tennis court, service area, and during his lunch hour, will serve tennis balls, trying to hit this cap or target for thirty minutes.

But we never hear of any match which has benefited from this practice, nor indeed of any Text-Book Man having made any competitive use of it. Text-Book Man is, in fact, one of the loneliest men in the world, a haunter of deserted darts boards and empty bowling alleys. A practiser of four-ball breaks on lonely croquet lawns, shut off by high walls. A lost figure seen sometimes, in the dusk, on the remotest hole of a golf course, standing behind a stack of golf balls, and rhythmically knocking them, one by one, with soft almost soundless smacks, up in the air over a bunker, on to the deserted green.

TYPE FOUR is perfectly represented by my friend Cropnorth. The key to Cropnorth is apparent almost as soon as he starts speaking. Cropnorth is a hero worshipper. He is fond of French films, goes to the Sadler's Wells ballet and the public performances of nineteenth-century piano concertos: but his real heroes are not Helpmann or Fernandel, Liszt or Clifford Curzon, but the man who is head of the averages in Lancashire League cricket, or Denis and Leslie Compton, or the Englishman

Moss-Jones would trace the romantic origin of the Tinsley Green marbles championship back to Armada days

who won the Diamond Sculls at Henley, 1950.

'He didn't care a damn,' Cropnorth was always saying, e.g. of a Lord's hero. 'He just came in and slogged the bowling as if he was playing the village postman. These chaps live in a time-world of their own. They actually see the ball one or even two seconds faster than anyone else.'

Later he will say about some of these hopelessly healthy-looking men (usually without any evidence, so far as I have been able to tell):

'I believe he's a very genial fellow. Sort of man who doesn't mind making a fool of himself. He signed my small nephew's autograph book just like that . . .

"Which way round do I hold the pen, sonny?" he said. Just a tiny touch – but he's supposed to keep everybody happy, like that.'

Then, later and always:

'Nothing in the slightest high hat about him. You'd never think, from his way of talking to you, that he'd scored more goals, in 1947, than any other Scotsman playing in League Football.'

TYPE FIVE is a worshipper not of the Player but the Place. The first entries in his New Year's engagement book will always be the games dates. Ryman is like that. Ryman is conventional in his choice of the perfect football place – the Arsenal ground at Highbury. But his first diary entry is January 6th, Rye Golf Course, the President's Putter. He will talk about the 'essence of golf' to be found in this competition on this course, the thin grass, dry with cold, clutching the sandy mountain range of the sea hole. For lawn tennis, he prefers the 'close-up pre-view' of the stars, just before Wimbledon, at Queen's Club. For rowing he prefers the regatta at Marlow, where it's all under your nose. Hen-

Above: Steeple-chasing at Lingfield. Near the camera, one of the finest amateur riders of his generation, the late Lord Mildmay. *Right:* Marlow Regatta, more than the fashions of Henley, attracts your true Gamesman

ley, yes, but the first two days only, not the end, when it's all cluttered up with female hats and middle-aged gentlemen bursting out of the trousers and blazers they were measured for in their youth.

For steeple-chasing he prefers Lingfield to any course, because you can see where you are, see the horses against the trees, when they're coming up the line, and the paddock and the bar and the tote are all together under your noses. For rackets he likes the foggy warmth of the Blackfriars Club, Manchester, in November. For cricket he prefers the Oval to Lord's, and Little Bardfield village green to either; but he always goes to the Oval in August, with dusty seats, and the smells and the old bits of newspaper and the ginger-beer bottles and the ice-cream refuse, and the boys rolling over each other in the waste spaces of the grass at the Vauxhall end.

All these places he will describe in detail, and mark the time of year by visiting each through the elaborate annual cycle which he has worked out. Neither illness nor work, birth, death nor marriage, have ever prevented him going to Aintree or Twickenham, Roehampton or the darts pub of 'Ypres Castle', Rye, for the dates, so delicately evocative of season and time, which each and every one of these places has stamped on his mind.

This man is very different of course from TYPE SIX, my friend E. D. C. Fittleworth. As his name and initials suggest, he is a games *player* above all, and certainly looks down on games watchers. He is a good games player — was in fact a quarter finalist in the squash rackets amateur in his twenties. And he frankly plays to win, and to win competitions. He will give you a friendly game of lawn tennis, but 'because of next week's match' he will be

Though Ryman may prefer golf at Rye, St. Andrews remains the headquarters of the Royal and Ancient game
Right: A sunlit green under the Curfew Tower of Windsor Castle, and a peaceful game of 'essential bowls'

'practising a new service', and forget the score in the little knock-around he is playing with you. He 'doesn't care about pots', but he polishes his little collection every week – this includes twelve spoons, for golf, and two big presentation models in electro-plate of golfers in cloth caps holding clubs the wire shafts of which have, in both cases, been lost by damage. He has three cups for winning the long jump and a soup tureen for representing Yorkshire at Badminton.

When playing golf, if he is not playing in a match, but a friendly, he will take, again, little notice of his opponent but will try to equal his own personal score-to-handicap, assessed by some system of adding up the strokes which is so complicated that he is always muttering and doing little sums on his card.

An unlovable but I suppose necessary characteristic of Fittleworth's is his knowledge of the rules. He specializes particularly in the rules of chess, croquet and golf. How many times have I heard Fittleworth say to me: 'You won't mind my saying so, but in a match that would have been my point,' – all because, so far as I can remember, I pressed down a worm-cast near a croquet hoop, or my dog sat down in a golf bunker.

Yet I would not say that Fittleworth's rules-consciousness was due to any malicious or unsporting desire to win by a trip. He takes actual delight in 'correct' playing, and I have heard him say 'beautiful interpretation of the rules' after what was in fact, unknown to him, a miscue of mine when, at snooker, my white ball was touching the object blue.

I have left for the last TYPE SEVEN because all types show some trace of his qualities, which are particularly and pervadingly British. The schoolboy who cannot memorise

'Interior of Tennis Court, Queen's Club, seen from the service-side: the numbers indicate the component parts of the hazard side.

1	is the	end-pent-house	9 is the	grille
2	,,	side-pent-house	10 ,,	last-gallery
3	,,	end-wall	11 ,,	second-gallery
4	,,	main-wall	12 ,,	door
5	,,	battery	13 ,,	first-gallery
6	,,	side-wall	14 ,,	line-opening
7	,,	tambour	15 ,,	half-court-line
8	,,	play-line		

That part of the court which is enclosed by the battery, the end-wall, the half-court-line, and the net is called the fore-hand court. The remainder of the court on the hazard-side is called the back-hand court.

Attention must be called to the floor, on which are painted certain lines.'

TENNIS - THE BADMINTON LIBRARY

the dates of James I will yet be able to tell you who played cricket for Kent in the season '39, and what Hammond's average was against Australia four years earlier. Games for the British is almost always games plus memories, or games plus games history.

Moss-Jones is the perfect example of this type. He really does seem to be under the dominion of the fascination of sport history. Whenever we pass the White City Greyhound Racing Stadium (on the way out to Moor Park for our golf) he invariably says 'I had a hound once – "a was outrun on Cots'l".' To forestall the invariable story, I remind him that I do in fact myself know the quotation, that the line occurs in Shakespeare's *Henry IV*, where somebody or other's hound was beaten at Captain Dover's racing games, on the Cotswolds.

In the same way, whenever Moss-Jones passes within ten miles of Rogate or Reigate, he will reconstruct for me the mediaeval hunting of the roe in these parts. 'Here', he will tell me, 'the "lymerer" would proceed along the "ringwalks" searching for the "slot" or "trace" of the deer, keeping an eye open for droppings or "fumes".'

Needless to say, Moss-Jones's favourite game was tennis – 'real' tennis, Royal tennis, but always to be called plain 'tennis'. He was always practising the basic tennis shot – even if he had a golf club in his hand it would suddenly become a racket and he would hold it for the tennis cut shot, the chop, half collapsing forward, knees sagging. He would tell grim stories of wrong behaviour at Hampton Court, of an opponent who played in shorts, of another who said 'good shot', instead of giving the ground a double tap with his racket.

Watching Moss play in one of those vast dark courts, with the mediaeval Norman names – tambour, dedans, chase – I did feel that a thousand ghosts were taking part in the game as well. And Moss had the power, also, of infusing all his game with this ghostly element of a Past. He couldn't play a simple game of shove-halfpenny without talking of shovel-board, its ancestor. He couldn't play golf without talking of Blackheath, with its imitation Scottish scenery, where golf was first brought to England by the Stuarts. And Buckingham Palace was to him the end of that Mall which Charles II railed off to play Pall Mall with his courtiers.

Have these types a common denominator? The easy answer is, I think, the wrong one – that the British take their games seriously.

Let us study this seriousness for a moment. For its essence let us look at some of the books on British Games of the eighties and nineties. The Badminton Library on lawn tennis for instance, or, better still, the Isthmian Library on croquet.

If lawn tennis appears here as a great new national force, croquet is given the status of an International and hostile Congress. In 1899 the croquet world, which had held complete sway through the seventies as an honourable and testing game for gentle people, was becoming conscious of a rival. 'The game of lawn tennis,' says the Isthmian, 'though excellent in every way, is on the decline...' It must and shall be on the decline, and to prove it, the rigours and grandeurs of croquet are set forth in 300 pages of rules and instructions, tables and characteristics of famous players.

The dedication sets the tone:

TO THE HONORARY SECRETARY OF THE
UNITED ALL-ENGLAND CROQUET ASSOCIATION
LIEUT-COLONEL
THE HONBLE. HENRY C. NEEDHAM
IN RECOGNITION OF THE
COURAGE WITH WHICH HE HAS UNDERTAKEN,
AND THE TACT AND EFFICIENCY WITH WHICH
HE HAS DISCHARGED,
DUTIES OF INCOMPARABLE DIFFICULTY AT A
CRITICAL PERIOD,
I DEDICATE THIS BOOK.

A 'critical period', for it had to be admitted that between 1884 and 1896, croquet had suffered a temporary decline. The lawn tennis scare had left its mark.

It is true that

'Captain Drummond, on his lawns at Petworth, continued to play croquet as if nothing had happened, and even held private tournaments with conspicuous success. His daugh-

Above: Croquet players, Roehampton Club, 1906. C. D. Locock, Silver Medallist, stands second from right
Left: '... More freedom out of doors: we may smoke ... but first and foremost let us have silence on the ground'

ter, Miss Maud Drummond, one of the most brilliant, and quite the most successful, lady player of the day, must have learnt all her croquet during this period.'

The spirit of croquet remained intact. But the chapter on 'Croquet Ethics' is given prominence as a firm reminder:

'Croquet is, and always has been, a game of the classes. It is, in the nature of things, very unlikely ever to become a pastime of the masses. At first sight one is tempted to conclude that, in these circumstances, any considerations on the subject of this chapter would be superfluous.'

Croquet-lawn manners are all-important. True,

'There is more freedom out of doors; we may smoke, we may even lounge – gracefully if we can – on the lawns and banks.'

But first and foremost, then, let us have

CROQUET
The stroke shown in this diagram, says Isthmian, is the 'Chop' or 'Block'. The only way to apply screw at our disposal, it is little used by experts. It retards rotation and the mallet embeds itself in the ground after the ball is struck.

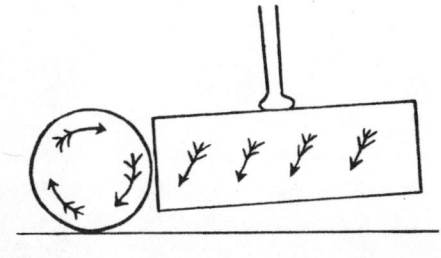

silence on the ground when an important match is afoot...

'If this were always done there would be less cause for complaint than now, unhappily, exists, on account of onlookers walking across the ground, engaging the players in conversation, making audible remarks about style, tactics, and other subjects of topical interest.'

Then of course there is the question of diet and training. The Isthmian recommends a cold tub, a gentle diet, followed by a few practice strokes with the mallet along a line on the carpet, and *not too much smoking*. The novice can scarcely conceive the strain of match play croquet:

'Leaving out of consideration the demands upon the nervous system, which are enormous, the physical, the purely muscular fatigue, the strain on back, arms, and lower limbs, would scarcely be credited by those who have never experienced it.'

Finally, the heroes and heroines of tournament play are paraded before our eyes, in the days when Wimbledon Championships meant croquet and nothing else. Mr. Trevor Williams, the celebrated front player (i.e. he played with his mallet in front of his legs, rather than at the side), Mr. C. D. Locock, and the Rev. Arthur Law, 'at one time the most brilliant exponent in England.' And there is Colonel Streeter. 'Everybody will remember,' says the Isthmian, 'the occasion when he said, "There's nothing for it but to go for it," and hooped diagonally across the lawn...'

'We take our games seriously – too seriously' – that is the natural conclusion, but I am convinced it is the wrong one. It is not games which the English are proud of, serious about, fanatics for: it is the character of Britain which, through games, they serve, admire, minister. Britons are rather loath to journey to Purbeck to admire the matchless view of heath and sea and weald from the cleft between Ballard and Nine Barrow Down. But they are perfectly prepared to motor 124 miles to the Swanage and Studland Golf Course and make this same view an incidental accompaniment to a game of golf.

The Englishman is diffident in his pride and passion for English History, but if he sees the Tudors as hunters and fencers, football players and experts in tennis, it somehow removes from history the savour of bookishness and dry fact.

How abstract and savourless are mathematics to the Briton, yet if they are about something – the laws of probability on a racecourse or the permutations and variations of football results – mathematics becomes right, good and admirable. In the same way 'Carthusian' feels a loyalty to the Englishness of his school and his old friends; but he will only admit to it in the name of games.

The great British game is to pretend to play games seriously. It is Britain, its heroes and history, its scenery and institutions, which we take in true earnest, with games as our cover and excuse.

Left: 1950: when Arsenal won the Cup Final for the third time and Littlewood's paid £92,000 for a penny

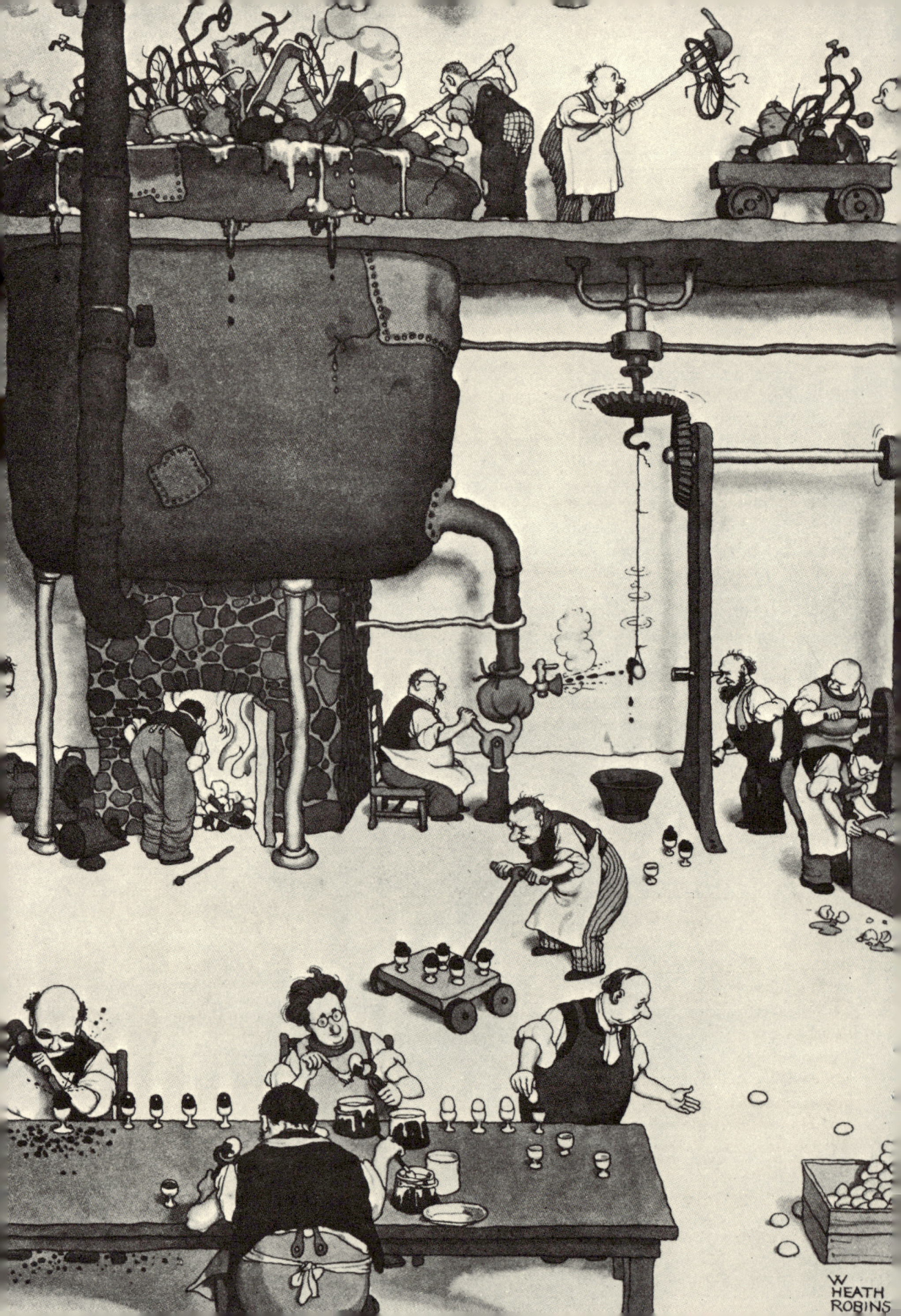

11
WE ARE AMUSED

By Paul Jennings

It may well be that the English are the most flippant people in the world, if by flippancy is meant a passionate refusal to talk seriously except on deathbeds and in debating societies (and not always then). When bombs were falling on London, people who might at any moment be buried under rubble and then drowned or burned were fond of telling each other this story. A London policeman, passing a graveyard during an air-raid, observed two skeletons, each carrying a tombstone. ' 'Ere, 'alf a minute,' he said, 'where you going with them stones?' 'That's all right, mate,' said one of the skeletons. 'Identity cards.'

This story, however, although it certainly illustrates the English boast that humour is our secret weapon, has about it a special London quality, some of the secret wryness, with a hint of the macabre, that sometimes makes a non-Londoner like myself feel that the Cockney is as mysterious and self-contained as the Etruscans were. If I were asked to produce one joke to typify English humour in general, I should certainly go to *Punch*, that ageless humorous weekly which somehow manages to be both brilliantly new and infuriatingly old; to attract old men in clubs (who are not so dull as you might think), and at the same time to insinuate surrealist cartoons for the young. I should need to look no farther than that first page of quips and comments headed, with typical obscurity, *Charivaria*; this is defined by the *Oxford Dictionary* as 'medley of sounds, hubbub (F., etym. dub.; prop. a serenade of pans, trays, etc., to unpopular person).' And I could do worse than choose this item:

' "Your cupboard must have been too moist or too hot. Do not, however, throw the jam away. Scrape off the mould and use it in jam tarts or puddings." — *Daily Paper*
  Then throw the jam away.'

There are, of course, elements in this jest that would amuse a Chinaman. For humour is a

Left: An armour-plating apparatus for eggs. One of Heath Robinson's many designs for industry

'The Three Graces in a High Wind in Kensington' by Gillray. During the formative period of modern England, the period which led up to the class split, a great deal of our creative humorous talent went into satire

tremendous intellectual leap, in which several ideas, which it would take quite a time to set forth in words, are fused in an instantaneous lightning flash. It is not necessary to be English to laugh at the idea of someone solemnly scraping the mould off mouldy jam and putting it into puddings; and an American, or even a Frenchman, might, in analysing this joke, agree that away down in one's subconscious there is an amusing picture of someone actually throwing jam away; one does not see him throwing the whole pot out of the window; somehow one sees him making flinging motions with jam-covered hands. All this is common human property. But there remain two specifically English elements. The first, and least fundamental, is a racial and linguistic one. It is simply that, to the English, 'jam' is a funny word. Go through the works of that brilliant daily humorist, 'Beachcomber' of the *Daily Express*, and you will find all through it magnificent blunt words

In Mrs. Grundy's reign, legs were thought not at all nice. Hence the table drapes and Puritan pantaloons

like pudding, glue, goloshes, treacle, jam, trombone...

Here, for instance, is Dr. Strabismus investigating the effect of music on industrial efficiency:

'The Doctor visited a large factory yesterday where goloshes are made and packed. He distributed violins to all the workers and told them to play something. Those who were able to master the instrument, owing to previous knowledge of it, quickly became engrossed in their own playing. Three sisters, who rendered Raff's Cavatina, failed to turn out a single golosh. On the other hand those who, after producing a few squeaks, abandoned the instrument, were distracted by the din made by their neighbours, and turned out goloshes so small or so shapeless that their time was wasted.'

At a further experiment, pianos at a jam factory became smeared with jam.

'After the luncheon interval a pip-inserter and a jar-lid-screwer essayed a duet. The black notes were clogged, and the attempt had to be postponed, while the instrument was swilled down with warm water.' Glass-blowers, 'after playing the trombone, found themselves blowing enormous and meaningless bulbs.'

It is anybody's guess why these words are funny to the English. Since they are nearly all non-Latin, it may simply be that we are inheriting the amusement of sophisticated French courtiers, after the Norman invasion, at the uncouth language of their Saxon hinds.

The second, and more fundamental, element in the mouldy jam joke is in its subtle combination of the earthy folk-laughter, this jam humour, the humour of the Lancashire comics, with the amused, slightly ironical laughter of the urban drawing-room; the laughter of the Oxford debate, of the Noel Coward play. 'Then throw the jam away' might easily be a Coward line. In the quintessential English humour there is always this agreeable balance between the natural and the cultivated. In *A Midsummer Night's Dream* (once described by a German music critic as 'slight piece' unworthy of the incidental music composed by Mendelssohn for it) we have the delightful Bottom and his gang of innocent artisans putting on their amateur tragedy for the Duke; and we have the comments of the sophisticated audience, like undergraduates at the local cinema. When Tom Snout the tinker says laboriously,

'and this same stone doth show
That I am that same wall; the truth is so',

Theseus whispers, 'Would you desire lime and hair to speak better?' and is answered, 'It is the wittiest partition that I ever heard dis-

Contrasts in unpredictable wonder. *Left:* Searle's age of innocence. *Above:* Mr. Bateman's unsinkable jam-jar lifeboat. When put to the test in 1831, it sank. The lid of the inventor's jar jammed and nearly choked him

course, my lord.' And when Hippolyta says, 'This is the silliest stuff that ever I heard', we seem to be right in our own day and age.

Yet there is no question of conflict between the two kinds of humour. As G. K. Chesterton remarked in an essay published some fifteen years after his death, '*A Midsummer Night's Dream* is a psychological study, not of a solitary man, but of a spirit that unites mankind.' And here we come to the heart of the matter. We of today are able to enjoy this double humorous life in Shakespeare, this oscillation between rustic and urban, sophisticated and simple, largely because of the implicit English belief that *both are good*. The fundamental English humour is shared by all classes, and anybody whose idea of us is derived purely from class-conscious jokes in Edwardian *Punch* is taking a very restricted view. The aristocrat stopped being an absolute figure of terror in England long before he did so anywhere else in Europe. To quote Chesterton again, 'The great and very obvious merit of the English aristocracy is that nobody could possibly take it seriously.' Sir Toby Belch and Sir John Falstaff can join the great democracy of English clowns because of one shared thing ... a distrust of intellectualism and academic theory. It is a commonplace that English philosophers are empirical and Continental ones are rationalist; and this slightly humorous withdrawal, this refusal to fit the facts of experience into a rigid intellectual framework, is characteristic of the inarticulate as well as the educated.

So far we have been considering a kind of ideal, abstract English humour. In actual historical fact it is not quite as simple as that, of course. There is something cyclic, a suggestion of the wheel having come full turn, in the ability of a modern Englishman to appreciate Shakespeare's classical English humour in quite the terms I have tried to describe. For, shortly after Shakespeare, England was squeezed in a fairly iron grip by the nearest thing to a rationalist philosophy that she has ever known – Puritanism. And Puritanism seized most tightly of all the artisan class, the unfortunate descendants of Snug the joiner and Flute the bellows-mender, those who were to become the industrial lower middle and working classes. As Puritanism broadened out into the Industrial Revolution, with its insistence on what were called the 'economic virtues' – dreary things like sobriety and thrift, and ploughing all one's profits back into t'mill instead of having a gay time – a rift grew between the common (and, increasingly, middle-class) man and that part of the gentility which shrank from the whole idea of industrialism, except for consenting to live on railway shares. Perhaps the farthest point of this separation was reached at the turn of the nineteenth century, with people like Oscar

Left: '*One for you, one for me . . .*'

THE GOLDEN KEY.

Mr. Montgomerie. "AH! MY DEAR BOYS, YOU'RE RIGHT. THE EXTENT TO WHICH OUR ENGLISH SYSTEM OF 'TIPPING' HAS GROWN IS SOMETHING MONSTROUS! WHY, I CAN ASSURE YOU—THAT—AT SOME OF THE BIG COUNTRY HOUSES I STOP AT, IT COSTS ME A TEN POUND NOTE TO GET OUT OF 'EM!" *Jones (to his neighbour, sotto voce).* "WONDER HOW MUCH IT COSTS HIM TO GET INTO 'EM?"

Above: *Punch*, vintage 1898; in the stately home life is different now. Below: 'Remind me in the morning to put up a notice making it clear that the 2s. 6d. trips round the Manor do not include bed and breakfast'

Wilde and Max Beerbohm at one end of the scale, Marie Lloyd (and later Gracie Fields) at the other. Here, for instance, is Max Beerbohm on the bicycle:

'The bicycle is complementary to the steam engine, doing for the horseless individual what the steam engine does for the community. It was as inevitable as it is unlovely, and I must put up with it. For the proletariat, it is not merely a necessity, but a great luxury. It gratifies that instinct which is common to all stupid people, the instinct to potter with machinery. In the hours of his leisure, if he be not riding, the cyclist is oiling his machine, or cleaning it when it is quite clean, or letting the air out of it for the simple pleasure of inflating it, or unscrewing it, or turning it upside down, or tapping it suspiciously with a pair of pincers.'

There was, of course, always *something* that could be described as national English humour. During the formative period of modern England, the period which led up to this class split – the eighteenth century – a great deal of our creative humorous talent went into satire, with men like Pope and Swift in literature, Hogarth, Gillray, Rowlandson in art. Cruikshank's cartoons epitomised the country's attitude to Napoleon. Nevertheless, by the end of the nineteenth century, English humour seemed to be completely sectionalised in class layers. It is only now, when we are many years removed from *Punch* jokes about housemaids wanting to learn the piano, when the classes have been thoroughly mixed up in two tremendous wars, that we are beginning to see that the division was not so profound after all.

For England has developed her own compromise version of the modern surrealist

A reproduction of a Boddery handbill. 'Ingenuity always kept him one step ahead of the thinking burglar.'

'Midsummer Night or NO Midsummer Night, I shall 'ave to report it'

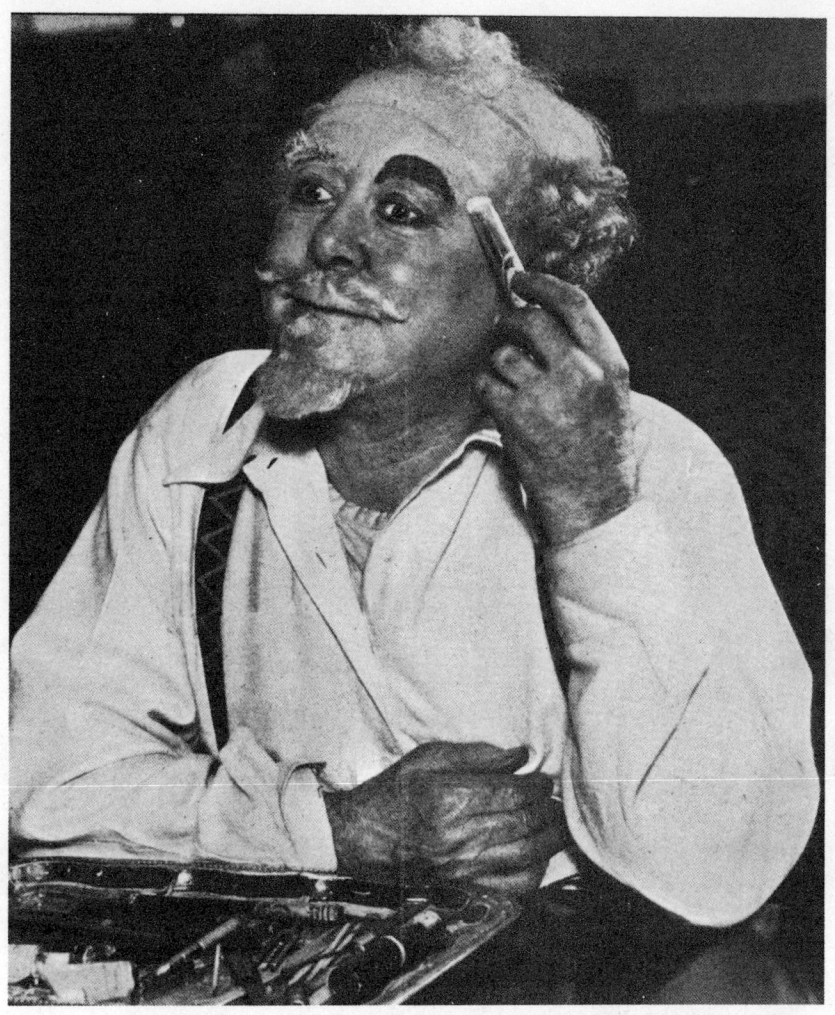

Above: Sir John Falstaff, here played by George Robey, has joined the great democracy of English clowns.
Left: On Midsummer Night, under an Emett moon, the world is something *other*, unaccountable, mysterious

humour of America, of the Marx brothers and Thurber. Today Oxford dons and canteen audiences can both laugh at a witty radio programme like *Take It From Here*, successor to the brilliant wartime *ITMA*. And one of the things that both agree on would have surprised those economic-virtues people – for they both agree that industrialism is *funny*. Look at Emett's curious trains. Look at the Beachcomber extract quoted above. Look at the remarkable industrial occupations in *Take It From Here*. I remember, for instance, the Fruit Lowerer – 'Naow, not Raiser, a Fruit Lowerer . . .' who wore a diving suit and was lowered into eighteen feet of *neutral* jam, carrying a suitcase full of strawberries, putting 'one here and one there as the fancy took him.' (Jam again!) We have named our machines and occupations as romantically as the Elizabethans named flowers. In the first few pages of the *Classification of Occupations 1950*, a vast book published by H.M. Stationery Office at 13/6d., there occur the following trades. Trolloper, Whammeller, Husbandman (in Wales), Thistle Spudder, Fang Manager, Hont Loader, Bogie Man, Thin Miner, Endless Rope Boy, Stone Head Lad, Rider on Top, Blaster, Bobby Lad, Tram Spragger, Transit Lad, Slummer, Snapper, Snapper-on, Snecker, Snibbler, Self-acting Dickie Boy, and Spragman.

Take It From Here: for millions, the organised excursion into lunacy is not a luxury but a weekly necessity

My own theory is that although the English invented industry they have never really believed in it, in the way that Americans do. Or if they have believed, it has been in what the deadpan scientists would doubtless consider the wrong way. There has been a tendency to believe that industry is *magic*, that nothing is too improbable in a machine world. It sometimes makes things a bit difficult for the humorist. For example, the advertisement reproduced on page 131 is part of an article I once wrote about a man who sold various devices which you could leave working noisily in your empty house to frighten burglars away. 'No scientific development,' I wrote, 'was overlooked by Boddery. Up to his death he was working on new techniques in invisible ray remote control. Last week I was shown over the Household Noises exhibit for this year's Ideal Home Exhibition, in which Boddery had taken a personal interest. As I approached a model house it was wrapped in a ghostly, dark silence. But when I got to within twenty yards and crossed a hidden ray which activated a selenium cell mechanism, the whole place suddenly burst into amazing life. I could have sworn there were three families there. One was singing glees in the front room, another was having an uproarious party somewhere at the back, a third was playing some mysterious game which involved running up and down the stairs.

A child was doing a bit of fretwork, and someone else was on the telephone. Dogs barked, babies squealed, people played "The Rustle of Spring" and gargled, and there was someone having a bath. Life was being lived very fully and richly in that house.'

Well, I got a lot of letters from people who asked me where these devices could be bought. One lady wrote to say that she thought the Bijou Domestic Bump and Tinkle Set would be sufficient for her needs, but was there a battery-operated model because she lived in the country and had no electricity? And someone else wanted to handle the German end of the business. Either the English think, deep down in their hearts, that industrialism is crazy like this, or else they are Against it. Even now British railwaymen insist on knockers-up, instead of having alarm clocks like everyone else. Even while they were inventing locomotives and Spinning Jennies, characters like Ned Lud were going round breaking up machines in inarticulate protest. We look at our countryside through the eyes of history, through the eyes of Jane Austen or Cobbett, so that the railway is something new and gawky, and, above all, funny.

Before industrialism, before the whole world became a sort of Newtonian machine, which we ourselves control in a bored sort of way, people had a sense of wonder. The world was something *other*, mysterious, unpredictable. Modern surrealist humour takes us away from this boredom into another world, the world of Thurber's card table. This, you will remember, had a gadget by which you could convert it into an ironing board; it was difficult to convert at first, but in the end it had to be left in the attic, where it could be heard bumping away all night as it changed itself back and forth. There is plenty of unpredictable wonder in *this* world, a lunatic place which men have created as a refuge from the repetitive dreariness of industrialism. The organised, technical joke, with its classical forms (the Englishman, the Irishman and the Scotsman etc.) was almost a one-act play, firmly rooted in humanity, but it is certainly a post-industrial thing. But in a gradual progression, by way of the class-conscious nineteenth-century jokes, humour has become a completely autonomous world of its own. The 'sense of humour' is regarded as an important qualification in a marriage partner, more important than other virtues more highly regarded by our forefathers. For millions, the weekly radio programme, the organised excursion into lunacy, is not a luxury but a necessity.

Now we are certainly indebted to America for this brushing away of the class-consciousness of our humour. But we have brought our own riches, as usual. The escape of American humorists into their fantasy world is more thorough-going, because it is an escape from a world more *committed* to machinery. The real English have been puckishly laughing at machinery, this newcomer, and all its social consequences, for some time now. But their humour is gentler because they are not seriously worried about it. I don't think the English are seriously worried about *anything*.

12
THE PAGEANT

By William Glenvil Hall

Visitors from overseas who have done no more than observe the sedate unconcern with which the officials tie up the cross-channel boat at Dover after the fuss and clamour at Calais: or watched the amazing taciturnity of the Island Race in buses and trains: or, hot from Paris, have remarked the steady refusal of our motorists to sound their horns and their 'No, after you, Cecil' attitude to each other in traffic, can hardly be blamed, I think, if they conclude that the British are a cold and undemonstrative people.

Nor, until they have seen us flock in our thousands to follow the antics of a baby bear, our pressmen wasting columns of precious newsprint on its doings: noted how eagerly we spend long hours of acute discomfort travelling to and fro for the privilege of swinging a rattle and wearing a coloured-paper cap in the appropriate place of battle for t' Cup: and have witnessed the bitterness with which in a land so small we can quarrel as to where a piece of stone shall rest, do they begin to realise that we are perhaps not so easy to classify as they had supposed at first sight.

What undoubtedly disconcerts them most is our silence in public, which they imagine is unfriendly indifference, and our belief in ourselves which they put down to arrogance.

Happily most of them soon discover that our reserve with strangers is not due to natural unsociability but to our love of personal independence, and that, though nothing can eradicate our faith in all things British, we don't expect them to share it if they prefer to deny the evidence of their own senses.

Nowhere do we demonstrate this passionate belief in our way of life more than in our attitude to the past. We hate to discard anything. Change for its own sake makes little appeal to us: it looks too much like breaking faith with those who have gone. When changes become imperative we will, if we can, adapt the old forms to new designs and, in spite of the Biblical warning against putting new wine into old bottles, not only glory in the operation but make it succeed.

As a result, more old customs have survived

Right: London's daily pageant: the Life Guards on parade

138 The St. George's Day procession of the Knights of the Garter, Britain's most ancient order of chivalry

and more ceremonial has been preserved in the United Kingdom than anywhere else on earth.

Some of these survivals, the Coronation Ceremony for one, with its solemn ritual and its mysteries of Divine Anointing and Dedication, are as essential today as ever they were. Others, though once essential to consolidate rights grudgingly conceded, are now only valuable as reminders that freedoms have had to be fought for. Others, large numbers of them, serve no useful purpose whatsoever and are only kept alive because they *are* old customs. All of them, so we feel, enlarge existence, add colour, pageantry and richness to life and help us to remember the hopes, the fears, the struggles and the victories of those who have preceded us.

This devotion of ours to the past helps, I think, to explain how it is that we can, to the astonishment of other nations, take part in many ceremonies which strike them as childish and even silly. For the curious thing is that although we have an intense dislike of making fools of ourselves in public we are capable of sharing in the absurdest of ceremonies without feeling the slightest embarrassment – provided they have the sanction of ancient usage.

It explains why staid City magnates, who would feel foolish at an Elks Convention or out of place in a Battle of Flowers, can without blushing parade the streets of London with nosegays in their fists, or sit, as a duly constituted Court, ankle-deep in aromatic herbs to ward off the plague, fortunately long since departed.

It explains why the Liverymen of the Worshipful Company of Vintners can still gravely go to church preceded by porters in clean aprons sweeping away with brand-new brooms non-existent litter from their path.

And it makes intelligible why the City Corporation can still solemnly pay over each year to the King's Remembrancer, for a piece of land near Chancery Lane upon which the Knights Templar used to joust, a quit-rent of six gigantic horseshoes and sixty-one nails, and tender at the same time a billhook and hatchet for another piece of land, never identified or occupied, near the town of Bridgnorth. These ceremonies have been enacted now for over 700 years, the City Solicitor on each occasion demonstrating the efficiency of the hatchet and billhook by chopping up a bundle of faggots into small bits.

It is of course just possible that I may be in error in assuming that these particular customs are kept alive out of sheer devotion to the past. In fact it may well be that they are perpetuated to extol the municipal enterprise of the Corporation in the field of sanitation and to exhibit to each succeeding generation the sanctity with which the City Fathers view a contract once entered into. I do not know. What I do know is that they add to the joy of life and I for one would hate to see them disappear.

The State Opening of Parliament by the Sovereign, at the beginning of each session, when he announces in person the legislation proposed for the months ahead, is both a splendid example of pageantry at its best and an act of the utmost constitutional importance.

This is one of the occasions when the King and Queen, attended by outriders, liveried footmen and Yeomen of the Guard, use the great carved and gilded coach drawn by eight cream-coloured horses for their journey to the House. The sight of it never fails to thrill the onlooker, however mechanically minded he may be, plain proof if proof be necessary, that whoever invented the story of Cinderella had the root of the matter in him.

The scene inside, after Their Majesties have arrived at the Victoria Tower, is one of great pomp and splendour and is perhaps, as the general public never sees it, worth describing in some detail.

At the head of the procession as it moves slowly along the Royal Gallery are the four Poursuivants, Rouge Croix, Rouge Dragon, Blue Mantle and Portcullis. They are followed by the high officers of state, the Keeper of the Privy Purse, the Lord High Chancellor in his gold-embroidered robes, the Lord President of the Council, the Lord Chamberlain and the Earl Marshal. Next, held aloft, comes the gold-sheathed Sword of State together with the Cap of Maintenance of red velvet and ermine. Then, fully robed, with pages in scarlet holding up their trains, come Their Majesties, the King wearing the Imperial Crown glittering with precious gems; the Queen shining with the loveliest jewels from the Tower, including the Cullinan diamond and the Koh-i-noor.

As they enter the House of Lords a fanfare is sounded and the assembly – Peers in their scarlet and ermine, judges in their full-bottomed wigs, bishops in their lawn sleeves and the Diplomatic Corps ablaze with Orders and Decorations – stands as the King leads the Queen to their thrones. The King bids the company be seated and a wait ensues while the Gentleman Usher of the Black Rod goes to the House of Commons to command their attendance.

Visitors from abroad, particularly those from the United States, find this pause in the proceedings very puzzling. It seems incredible to them that we cannot arrange for members of Parliament to be ready in their places when the King arrives and thus avoid what looks remarkably like gross discourtesy to him. Americans, they say, wouldn't dream of keeping their President waiting in this way.

To adopt this suggestion would mean to begin with a departure from custom which was obviously old when Queen Elizabeth was on the throne. For an account has come down to us of a similar ceremony enacted one April day 380 years ago when she attended the House behind 'the golden-sheathed sword, the jewelled Cap of Maintenance' and her high

Still mindful of Guy Fawkes, Yeomen of the Guard search Parliament's vaults before each State Opening

officers of state in their 'robes, mantles, circots and hoods'. 'There she sat', the account continues, 'in princely and seemly sort, under a high and rich canopy; the Lords spiritual and temporal before her, ranged in order due, and the judges on the woolsacks in the midst. Notice then that the Queen was on the throne was given to the knights, citizens and burgesses of the House of Commons. They, thereupon, repairing to the Parliament House were let in and stood together behind the Bar at the lower end. The Queen then rose from her regal seat, and with a princely grace and singularly good countenance, spake a few words, thus: "My right loving Lords, and you our right faithful and obedient subjects, We in the Name of God, for His Service, and for the safety of this State, are now assembled, to His glory, I hope; and I pray that it may be to your comfort and to our common quiet and to yours and all ours for ever." '

To have the Commons already assembled at the Bar would also mean the end of another custom which, though not so old by the best part of a century and almost pure comedy from start to finish, is fraught with deep significance for those who love to remember how far democracy has travelled.

Black Rod has by now reached the Commons. They have been on the look-out for him and are indeed pleased to see him, although they shew it by slamming the door in his face with such violence that the noise can be heard by those waiting in the Lords nearly a hundred yards away.

Black Rod, undeterred by this rebuff, which frankly he expected, proceeds to hammer three times on the door and is not surprised

All over Britain, on the Fifth of November, children have their own ways of celebrating the Gunpowder Plot

The Lord Mayor's Show. *Above:* A new Lord Mayor rides in his golden coach to take the oath before the Lord Chief Justice. *Below:* A pack of hounds comes to London to take part in the City's most famous pageant

to see the barred wicket open and the eyes of the Serjeant-at-Arms scrutinising him. Reassured by what he sees, for Black Rod has brought no soldiers with him, the Serjeant flings wide the door. Thereupon, Black Rod, bowing to left and to right, marches unhindered down the floor towards Mr. Speaker and delivers his message.

Immediately he has departed, the Serjeant-at-Arms lifts the mace from the table, Mr. Speaker steps down from his chair, and the faithful Commons troop off without more ado to the Lords where, crowded at the Bar, they listen to the Speech from the Throne being read.

Slamming the door in Black Rod's face, as I have already indicated, is a comedy, but a comedy charged with meaning. Few acts surely are simpler to perform and few more expressive of intention than shutting the door in a visitor's face, and the fellow who suggested it in this connection was obviously inspired. For it symbolises beyond question the right of the Commons to exclude the Sovereign or his emissary from their Chamber.

Their right to conduct business in their own way and time is emphasised the same day by a device equally simple. Having returned from the Lords, the Clerk announces the Title of a non-existing Bill – For the Better Protection Against Clandestine Outlawries – after which token gesture of defiance, for the Speech has been prepared by the Government and not by the King, they settle down to discuss its contents.

Black Rod, the emissary of the King on this occasion, is both a member of the Lord Chamberlain's department and an officer of the Most Noble Order of the Garter. This, the oldest order of chivalry in England, was instituted by Edward III to revive the spirit of the Round Table and 'to increase virtue and valour in the hearts of the nobility'.

Its name, and the fact that part of the insignia of the Order is a jewelled garter, has led to the popular belief that it was instituted following an episode at Edward III's Court, but Joseph Pote in his *History and Antiquities of Windsor*, published in 1749, scathingly dismisses this as 'remote from the truth and unsupported by the least authority.'

'It must be observed', he says, 'common fame has departed from the truth and given an amorous account of the institution of the most noble Order and a vulgar opinion has prevailed that at a solemn ball in King Edward's Court the garter of Joan, Countess of Salisbury casually falling off in dancing, the Prince hastily took it up from the ground; at which his nobles and courtiers smiling and giving it an amorous turn, the King taking notice of their sportive humour immediately replied in French, "Honi soit qui mal y pense", and added that in a short time they should see that garter advanced to so high honour as to account themselves happy to wear it.'

The ribbon of the Order was, I am told, formerly worn round the neck, the badge of St. George, its patron saint, coming in the middle of the breast. It is now displayed across the chest, a change, according to gossip, resulting from an accident which might easily have happened to any one of us *if* we were members of this Most Noble Order and if, *too*, we dressed by candlelight.

The story is that the Duke of Richmond who flourished in the reign of George III had the misfortune to singe the ribbon of his Order in the flame of a candle standing on his dressing table. As it was impossible at that time of night to get another piece he, with praiseworthy ingenuity, fixed the undamaged portion diagonally across his chest. The King, so runs the tale, was so struck by the look of it worn in this way that he made the change permanent.

Our love of old customs and our resolve to continue them at all costs could hardly be better illustrated than in the tenacity with which we cling to survivals, some of them very trivial indeed, in that citadel of democracy, the House of Commons itself.

It is, for example, customary for a piece of tape, specially looped, to be hung from each Member's peg in the cloakroom. Put there originally to hold swords, they nowadays carry nothing more lethal than an umbrella, but this does not prevent them from being carefully renewed at the beginning of each session.

It was a strict rule in the old days that no-one speaking from one of the front benches should put so much as a toe over the edge of the narrow strip of carpet running along the floor at his feet. This custom was instituted to prevent Members in the heat of debate from reaching each other with their rapiers. Except for the ceremonial sword carried by the Serjeant-at-Arms, no weapon of any kind is now allowed in the Chamber but this fact does not prevent Mr. Speaker, vocally supported by an outraged House, from insisting upon rigid observance of this ancient regulation.

Only wholehearted devotion to the past can surely account for our loving adherence to survivals like these which are perpetuated without question or complaint. It is true that occasionally a newly-elected Member arrives, firmly resolved in advance not to succumb to the atmosphere of the place, only to find himself as the days pass becoming as devoted as the rest to these and to other harmless but picturesque remnants of continuous procedure handed down by their predecessors.

How many people I wonder know that Mr. Speaker has a state coach of his own? Actually it is older than the King's. Whenever he sallies forth in it he is entitled to an escort of one lifeguardsman and four mounted policemen and, perhaps more useful in these days for it weighs $2\frac{3}{4}$ tons and has no brakes, the right to call upon Messrs. Whitbread the brewers for the loan of two horses.

This reliance on Messrs. Whitbread for motive power is an up-to-date example of how a custom can grow up. For it seems clear to me that if Mr. Shaw-Lefevre, who became Speaker in 1839, had not been a partner in that firm and if during his tenure of office there had been no occasion to use the coach, this particular custom would not have become established.

Westminster Hall, the oldest part of the Palace, has been the setting for many historical events. Much pageantry has been enacted down the centuries beneath its magnificent hammer-beamed roof. It was here that Guy Fawkes and his confederates were sentenced, and afterwards hanged, drawn and quartered just outside in Old Palace Yard.

British youth has of course its own particular ways of celebrating the famous exploit of Guy Fawkes, but it has always surprised me that Parliament, an institution for which he undoubtedly had some distaste, should go out of its way to keep his memory green and, incidentally, put ideas into the heads of evilly disposed persons, by having the vaults of the Palace searched by Yeomen Warders of the Guard before the opening of each session.

Yet, so it is. Lanterns burning candles are still used on these underground expeditions although the passages traversed are brightly lit by electricity. The reassuring tidings that the cellars are clear of intruders, once conveyed to the Monarch by a mounted trooper, is now telephoned to the Palace by the Vice-Chamberlain of the Household.

The Yeomen of the Guard, or Beefeaters, who carry out this search are themselves members of a Corps which has existed for over 500 years. Established in Tudor days to 'guard the Body of our Lord the King', day and night, they alone had the job of making the King's bed, obviously a task with more to it than occurs to the modern mind. I am assured by a friend, whose knowledge in this direction is profound, that the assignment of this duty to them was in no way connected with Henry VIII's marriage to Anne Boleyn. For as every schoolboy knows, it was her unfortunate habit of munching biscuits during the night which finally decided Henry to get rid of her. The duties of the Yeomen are now largely confined to attendances at state functions. One of the many colourful ceremonies at which they assist is that of the yearly distribution of Maundy Money. This ceremony, a survival of the old ecclesiastical custom which ordained that the Sovereign should wash the feet of as many old men as the years of his age and afterwards present them with money, meat and clothes, is held in West-

Above: The Archdruid at Cardiff Eisteddfod. The Common Riders of Hawick, in Scotland. *Below:* Southampton celebrates its 500th birthday at the 'Red Lion'. Dagenham pipers, a new tradition in a new town

Housewives of Olney round the last bend in the 500th year of their pancake race. In 1949 a challenge came from the ladies of Liberal, Kansas. This 415-yard sprint has now become an annual transatlantic fixture

minster Abbey on the Thursday before Easter.

The washing of feet has been discontinued since the middle of the eighteenth century, although well before that monarchs had begun to take the precaution of having the feet of those chosen washed in advance in warm water and herbs by Yeomen of the Laundry. Special coins are now minted for the occasion. These, tucked into coloured purses with girdle-strings, are borne into the Abbey by one of the Yeomen on an enormous silver-gilt dish.

The lineaments of the past are, as may be supposed, easily discernible in the City of London where, the onward march of democratic processes notwithstanding, the Corporation still exercises considerable dignities and privileges some of them dating back to Anglo-Saxon times. Within the Corporation the Livery Companies, successors of the early Guilds, some of which, like the Tallow Chandlers', have long since been deflected from the glories of their ancient crafts, continue to exercise their 'free and undoubted privilege' to elect the Lord Mayor, though their choice is, and always has been since the time of King John, subject to the King's ratification.

It was this journey to Westminster, accompanied by a throng of boisterous apprentices, to receive the monarch's approval which developed into the Lord Mayor's Show. The quality and indeed the popularity of this event had varied greatly down the years, the yearly displays differing, like the stars, in magnitude. They probably reached their nadir during the fifties of the last century. In that decade the newspapers record that the processions had become little more than a string of private

A mysterious 11th-century Horn Dance is still performed at Abbots Bromley. Twelve men in antique dress, some with reindeer horns, dance throughout a September day. No-one knows the origin of this bizarre caper

carriages interspersed with a military band or two and slightly diversified by a few men in armour from Astley's. In 1856 the water pageant was held for the last time and the following year the Court of Aldermen decided to sell the City Barge. Today the Show has regained much of its one-time splendour and seems less likely than ever to fulfil the prophecies of its early death made not so many years ago.

If, as Ralph Waldo Emerson once observed, 'the Middle Ages still lurk in the streets of London', they also most assuredly persist in many other parts of Britain to a far greater extent than many imagine. It is not difficult to understand how it is that Norwich, York, Winchester, and other old cities retain so many of their old customs. For with them tradition is deep-rooted and civic pride has everything outwardly to sustain it in ancient buildings, mediaeval ceremonies and muniments.

But the persistence, and in some cases the revival, of old customs on the countryside is an interesting phenomenon. For there if anywhere one would expect the mechanisation of farming and transport, and the arrival of wireless and the cinema to have destroyed many old usages which in the nature of things normally depend for their survival on the community which practises them being turned inwards upon itself and living isolated from the outside world. Yet they live on in spite of the fact that many of them were originally connected with feast days now no longer universally celebrated, or with the departure of winter, not now so ardently looked forward to as it was in the days of rushlights and before the coming of glass into common use.

In olden days people confessed their sins to the priest at Shrove-tide in preparation for Lent and afterwards gave themselves over to carnival and games and the eating of pancakes. At Olney in Buckinghamshire all three are still combined in a 500-year-old custom which takes the form of a pancake race on Shrove Tuesday. There on that day at the first peal of the pancake bell from the tower of the fourteenth-century church those taking part begin to make their pancakes. This task completed, they hurry with them still in the frying pan to the Market Square where, at a given signal, they run to the church a distance of over 400 yards tossing their pancakes three times on the way once at least as they dash up the path to the church door.

Many of these country survivals are folk-dances with age-old jingles to match the steps. Most of the Floral Dances are of this kind though they have probably come down to us by a different route from the Maypole dancing of Merrie England days.

Modern dances recognise no frontiers which, as most of them are foreign concoctions and consist mainly of shuffling, is a great pity. For none of them can equal the English ballet for grace and expression or our native folk-dances for pageantry. The most English of these measures is without doubt the Morris dance. No mediaeval festival was reckoned complete without it particularly when it was danced, as it often was, in flamboyant costumes ornamented with bells tuned to different notes in the scale. Suppressed, as so many good things unfortunately were with the bad, in Cromwellian times it is now, like Maypole dancing, being revived by enthusiasts in many areas.

Nothing of course could suppress the Irish jig, the only national dance Ireland seems to have produced, or the Highland Fling of Scotland with which it has so much in common. The thrust and warmth of the foursome reel or the sword dance is a sight to stir the blood, all the more colourful since the dividing-out of the tartans between the clans has popularised the kilt.

Scotch Rhapsody in English ballet. Ashton's *Façade*
Left : The reel is danced wherever the Scots gather

The Welsh seem to have had no ambitions in this direction unless theirs were the original little hills that skipped. Local patriotism in their case has been fostered on music, singing and poetry. Unlike the bagpipes, the harp apparently needs no extraneous aid to distract and keep the onlooker happy. Bards and minstrels have flourished down the centuries in Wales. So much so in fact that, in the sixteenth century, the 'intollerable multitude of vagrants and idle persons naming themselves minstrelles, rithm's and barthes' became such

'I know that I have the body but of a weak and feeble woman: but I have the heart and stomach of a king.' This is the spirit of Britain's women – the spirit of Elizabeth in the past, in the present, and in the future

a nuisance that Queen Elizabeth, to abate the scandal and to give the national urge for expression in this direction a legitimate outlet, ordered an Eisteddfod to be held at Caerwys.

At no period of our history has pageantry in its many guises come to such full flowering as in the great age of Elizabeth. She was the first purely English sovereign and it was during her reign that the drama reached its greatest height in the hands of Shakespeare, and the masque, a combination of music, dialogue, scenery and dancing, attained a vogue never since equalled.

It is surely no mere flight of fancy to see a definite connection between these things and the actions and attitude toward life of the men and women of that time. Is it straining credulity too far to believe that so rich a feast must have influenced and influenced profoundly the outlook of those who lived in that epoch? For it was then that men took to the sea in a big way – the one remaining outlet for those of adventurous spirit; then that an English Admiral had the iron nerve to finish a game of bowls before engaging a mighty foe; then that men and women, with all their faults and weaknesses, appear to have met the crises of life with a courage and a noble bearing never before so commonly attained. 'I come amongst you', said Elizabeth to her troops gathered at Tilbury to resist the Spanish Armada, 'not for my own recreation or disport, but resolved in the midst of battle to live or die amongst you all, to lay down for my God and my Kingdom and my people, my honour and my blood even to the dust. I know that I have the body but of a weak and feeble woman: but I have the heart and stomach of a king, and of a king of England too.' And it was this same spirit that surely gave Raleigh, some years later, the courage to say, when asked which way he would like to place his head on the block, 'What matter it how the head do lie as long as the heart be right.'

The aim of pageantry it has been said should be to arouse civic pride, increase the community spirit, instil a love of the beautiful and inculcate a desire to emulate the achievements of the past. What it certainly should not do is to stimulate an aggressive nationalism, be simply an excuse for a display of military force or foster an arrogant attitude towards other nations.

It is not perhaps for me to say how Britain, devoted as her people are to pageantry in all its forms, stands up to these tests. What does appear clear is that, with all our love of pomp and circumstance, pageantry with us has never taken the form of great displays of armed might. We have never been addicted to the holding of great military parades. The vast array of men goose-stepping with endless banners through Nuremberg or the miles-long processions of troops, tanks and guns across the Red Square, find no echo here and would probably only bore our people if they were attempted. Military pageantry in this country takes other patterns – the Tattoo, the Tournament and Trooping the Colour.

The Colour is trooped once a year on the King's birthday. Held as it is on the Horse Guards Parade, with the weathered grey buildings on one side and the peaceful lake amid the trees and flowers on the other, the display is in the nature of a family party rather than an exhibition of military force. For on these occasions the King is accompanied by Princess Elizabeth and his brothers, with Queen Elizabeth and their grandchildren looking on from a nearby balcony.

Here, to the delight of the spectators of all ages, the Brigade of Guards, resplendent in their red tunics and bearskins and led by their massed bands, the sun glinting from their instruments and shining on the gold of their facings, march and counter-march, in slow time and in quick, with a precision and symmetry splendid to behold. Would that all displays were as colourful and as harmless as this.

As the reader will have realised from the other contributors to this book, Britain has, in spite of her devotion to the past and her dislike of change, taken her full share in the advances made by mankind down the centuries.

Paradoxical though it may sound, there can be little doubt that the solid and enduring qualities of her achievements in so many fields – the arts, science, invention, industry – have been greatly helped by her staunch devotion to tradition and to the tenacious way in which she has clung to ancient manners and customs. It can be argued with I believe great force that her record would not have been so outstanding had she not had the wit and inclination to draw much of her inspiration from the stored lore and knowledge of the ages.

For, like her native oaks, she has been made immeasurably stronger by striking her roots so deep.

ACKNOWLEDGEMENTS

The publishers gratefully acknowledge the courtesy of the following who have granted permission to reproduce pictures in this book:

Derek Adkins, p. 29, (two pictures)
Adprint Colour Service, pp. 36, 56, 59, top and centre; 76, 81, 84
Aerofilms Ltd., endpapers, pp. 8, 19, 21
The Badminton Library, pp. 110, bottom; 111, 118
Baron, p. 149
Cecil Beaton and Associated Press, p. 150, centre
Black Star, p. 16
The Curators of the Bodleian Library, p. 97
N. K. Branch, p. 63
Bill Brandt, pp. 17, 41, bottom
The B.B.C., pp. 100, 134
The Trustees of the British Museum, pp. 10, 35, 96
Charles E. Brown, pp. 12, bottom; 73
Howard Byrne, pp. 137, 148
Camera Talks, p. 23
J. Allan Cash, p. 45
Central Office of Information, pp. 38, 47, 53, top left; 54, 62, 65, 67, 74, 94, top (Crown Copyright reserved)
Central Press Photos, pp. 66, 70, 77, 79, 142, bottom; 150, right
John Chettleburgh, p. 147
The Council of Industrial Design and Messrs. Stevens and Williams, p. 47
The Croquet Association, p. 111
Lord De L'Isle and Dudley, V.C., p. 150, left
The Curator of the Examination Schools, Oxford, p. 98, left
The *Field*, cover photograph and p. 15
Fox Photos, endpapers, pp. 13, 31, 32, 33, 43, 51, top left and right; 61, 82, top; 83, 109, 116, 133, 140
Future, pp. 6, 53, top right; 58, top; 59, 108
G.B. Instructional Ltd., p. 89
Giles and Express Newspapers, p. 130, bottom
Douglas Glass, p. 75
Graphic Photo Union, pp. 113, 119, 122, 138
Harland and Wolff Ltd., p. 69
Illustrated, pp. 52, 60, 145, top right
Imperial War Museum, p. 12, top
Karsh and Camera Press, p. 102
Keystone, pp. 11, 24, 110, top; 145, bottom left and right
Lynx Copyrights Ltd., pp. 125, 129

Angus McBean, p. 105, top
The M.C.C., p. 108
The Masters of the Bench of the Honourable Society of the Middle Temple, p. 76
Mirrorpic, pp. 68, 82, bottom; 136, 141
The National Maritime Museum, p. 6
The Trustees of the National Portrait Gallery, pp. 86, bottom right; 87, right; 98, right
George Newnes & Co. Ltd., p. 106
Paramount Pictures, p. 104
The Parker Gallery, p. 6
Michael Peto, pp. 14, 22, 42
Photochrom, p. 28
Pictorial Press, p. 64
Picture Post Library, pp. 7, 20, 30, 41, top; 46, (two pictures); 50, (two pictures); 51, bottom; 53, bottom; 86, top and bottom left; 87, left; 88, 90, (two pictures); 92, left; 93, 95, 101, 103, 112, 126, 127
Planet News, p. 151
The Proprietors of *Punch*, pp. 130, top; 132, 135
Oliver Robinson, Esq., p. 124
Rolls Royce Ltd., p. 72, (two pictures)
The Director of the Science Museum, South Kensington, pp. 85, 92, right (Crown Copyright reserved)
Ronald Searle and Express Newspapers, p. 128
Sport and General Press Agency, pp. 114, 115
Stoke-on-Trent City Museums, p. 59
W. Suschitzky, p. 120
Lord Tedder and Leslie Durbin, p. 55
Topical Press, pp. 34, 94, bottom; 142, top; 145, top left; 146
Val Doone, pp. 25, 26, 27
The Director of the Victoria and Albert Museum, pp. 44, 48, 49
Walker's Galleries Ltd., pp. 37, 39
Josiah Wedgwood & Sons, Ltd., pp. 58, (two pictures); 59, bottom
Woburn Studios, p. 117
The text of the handbill on p. 131 originally appeared in *Oddly Enough* by Paul Jennings, published by Messrs. Reinhardt & Evans